Family Sanctuary

Restoring the Biblically Hebraic Home

-Cover Photo by Jim Ransdell

Restoration Foundation

Restoration Foundation is an international, transdenominational, multicultural teaching and publishing resource to the Christian community. This ministry features a network of scholars, church leaders, and laypersons who share the vision for restoring the Hebrew foundations of the Christian faith, promoting the unity of the Spirit among believers, and returning the church to a biblical relationship of loving support for the international Jewish community and the nation of Israel.

We publish ***Restore!*** magazine, a high-quality journal that features theological balance and scholarly research. ***Restore!*** helps Christians recover their Hebraic heritage while strengthening their faith in Jesus. We also publish and distribute ***Golden Key Books***, a publishing effort that focuses exclusively on producing and marketing books and other materials that teach the various aspects of Christianity's Jewish roots.

We maintain an inspirational and informative Internet web site: www.restorationfoundation.org. Through this medium, we make much of our material available free of charge to people around the world. Entire issues of ***Restore!*** and volumes of ***Golden Key Books*** can be studied here.

We are pleased to offer to all denominations and fellowships the teaching of our gifted scholars for conferences, seminars, and other instructional forums that can be tailored to each individual setting.

Our team of ***Golden Key Partners*** around the world help us translate these various parts of our expansive vision into the programs that touch the lives of thousands. We invite you to join us as full partners in this teaching and publishing ministry. Together we are making a difference in the world by restoring Christians to their biblically Hebraic heritage, by eradicating Judaeophobia and anti-Semitism, by supporting Israel and the international Jewish community, and by encouraging unity among those who share this vision.

For information about Restoration Foundation, ***Restore!*** magazine, ***Golden Key Books***, ***Living Emblems***, ***Beth Midrash***, conference speakers, and ***Golden Key Partnerships***, contact us at the address below.

Restoration Foundation
P. O. Box 421218
Atlanta, Georgia 30342, U.S.A.
(678) 615-3578
www.RestorationFoundation.org

Family Sanctuary

Restoring the Biblically Hebraic Home

John D. Garr, Ph.D., Th.D.

GOLDEN KEY BOOKS
Restoration Foundation
P. O. Box 421218
Atlanta, Georgia 30342, U.S.A.

Published by Restoration Foundation
P. O. Box 421218, Atlanta, GA 30342
ISBN 0-9678279-8-1

Printed in the United States of America

All Scripture verses are quoted from the
Authorized King James Version
unless otherwise noted.

To my loyal friend and
colleague Dwight Pryor
and in loving memory
of his valiant wife,
Jeanette, who, like
Sarah of old,
epitomized Hebraic
hospitality by opening
the Pryor family
sanctuary to Pat and
me and blessing us with
faith and love.

TABLE OF CONTENTS

Introduction

Everyone needs sanctuary, a place of peace and safety, a place of blessing and affirmation, a place of sanctity and security. These are the functions for which God designed the home from time immemorial. Through the centuries, however, persistent and unrelenting attacks have been made upon the most fundamental unit of both society and the church. Hellenization, Latinization, and secularization have rendered the modern Christian home a mere shadow of its biblical ideal.

God's design for the home, however, has always been and will always be the same. It is perfectly clear when we return the family and home to the matrix from which it emerged in a truly biblical restoration. It is not enough, however, to call simply for "biblical" restoration. The term *biblical* has become so diluted that it has been virtually eviscerated of meaning. In order for true biblical order to be restored, a return to the "biblically Hebraic" must take place. The unfortunate truth about most faiths in today's world is that they *claim* to be biblical but they fall far short of *being* biblical.

The problem is that practically all societies and people groups have read their own concepts and cultures into the Bible rather than drawing out from the Holy Scriptures the truths that have always been there. The church's approach to the Holy Writ has been ignorant at best and disingenuous at worst. When interpreting the Bible, Christians have engaged in eisegesis rather than exegesis by injecting their preconceived notions into Scripture rather than extracting from the text what it clearly says.

Texts without contexts have become pretexts. The grammar of the Scriptures (the Hebrew language of the first testament and Hebrew thought underlying the Greek language of the second testament) has been largely minimized. Likewise, the history and culture of the people through whom and to whom the sacred texts were committed have been ignored. Entire theologies have been based upon a "criterion of dissimilarity" in which texts in the Apostolic Scriptures that have clear connections with the Hebrew Scriptures have been dismissed as not being the authentic words of Jesus and the apostles but the work of subsequent redactors. The very idea has given rise to a Christianity that has been wrenched from its moorings and set adrift in a maelstrom of non-biblical–even anti-biblical–traditions, secular humanism, and demonic perversion.

In order to restore society to a "biblical" basis, the church must first restore the Hebraic roots of the Christian faith. This is especially true in the important arena of human relationships. God's perspectives on family and the home can never be understood without a renewal of the Hebraic foundations which God himself established for this core element of human existence.

A complete rethinking of the issues of family and home is necessary. Ideas founded in Greek philosophy and in various polytheistic and monistic religions must be abandoned. If today's society is to be saved from implosion because of the destruction of its nuclear unit (the family) a return to biblically Hebraic understanding must occur. Nothing short of a Hebraic restoration will suffice.

God's Word works! What God has said will outlast everything that exists. "Heaven and earth will pass away, but my words will never pass away," Jesus declared. What God said about family and home is ultimate truth, and God's Word is the only thing that will endure. Since God dynamically modeled among the Jewish people his instructions regarding society's fundamental unit, it is to the Jewish people and the Hebrew Scriptures that the church and society must look for understanding that will renew the biblical home and bring health and vitality to society at large.

Trying to fabricate a program that will somehow accommodate the modern notion of family by obliquely incorporating biblical terminology into sociological or psychological categories will only result in furthering the disaster. A thin veneer of religiosity over societal definitions of family will not suffice. Syncretism is not the answer.

It is for this reason that I have undertaken the research and writing of this volume. It is my understanding that recovering the Hebraic foundations of the Christian faith is a golden key that unlocks the treasures of Holy Scripture and enriches the lives of believers. In no area of life could this be more true than in the family and the home.

I wish to thank my faithful colleague Dr. Karl Coke for his ongoing insightful teaching on the primacy of the family as the institution for spiritual growth and maturity for Christian believers. My colleagues Dr. Marvin Wilson and Dwight Pryor have also imparted superb teaching on this important issue.

I wish also to express my appreciation to my dear friends Dr. Charles and Luellen Bryant-Abraham for their careful reading and evaluation of the manuscript and for their insightful and helpful suggestions. Judy Grehan has also been an invaluable asset with her thoughtful observations and careful copy editing of this book. My dear Israeli friend, Zvi Zachor, has fulfilled an important role in promoting and marketing my books, including this volume.

A host of other friends have joined together with Pat and me as a family in community, lending their support, prayers, and advice as we seek to provide quality, theologically sound, and conceptually balanced materials on which individuals and faith communities can build solid lives and ministries. It is a challenge that we do not take lightly, nor do we imagine in our wildest dreams that we could do it alone. Our laterally connected network of scholars and leaders gives us mutual accountability, both academically and spiritually, and for that we are exceedingly grateful.

I believe that as you read this volume, you will be challenged intellectually and spiritually to consider new insights on what I believe are restored biblical and historical positions on some of the most important issues in life, those that impact the family and the home. I pray that they will assist you in establishing the sanctity of your home and building and maintaining your family sanctuary.

Fraternally in Messiah
John D. Garr, Ph.D., Th.D
Sukkot, 2003

Chapter 1

Society's Heart and Soul

THE INDISPENSABLE FAMILY

Sanctuary! A respite of safety and security. Repose in loving, affirming relationships. Relief from stress and rest from labor. A retreat to sanity in a world of madness. A refuge for spiritual renewal, growth, and development. The biblically Hebraic home is God's provision for all of this and more!

Unfortunately, however, these are not descriptions of the average home in dysfunctional Western culture. During the past few decades, revisionist attempts have been made to redefine both the family and the home. Men with political agendas designed on societal or world domination have made savage efforts to restructure the understanding of the home or to destroy it altogether. The nuclear family is under heavy attack from demonic societal forces that threaten its demise.[1]

Still, the family remains the fundamental building block of society, and the home is society's heart and soul. Healthy homes produce healthy societies. When societies have strong and mutually affirming bonds in the home, a general sense of security provides an atmosphere conducive to personal growth and the resultant courage to strive for excellence.

On the other hand, when the bonds of family are not valued and strengthened, a general sense of insecurity arises, resulting in malaise and irresponsibility. Dysfunctional or non-functional homes produce societies marked by either anarchy or autocracy. When societies depart from the fundamental model of social interaction that the Creator designed the home to be, fundamental morality suffers, and general societal disintegration occurs.

DYSFUNCTIONALITY AND DEMOLITION

The mad and maddening quest for "success" that has glorified–even deified–individual accomplishment in the modern and post-modern worlds has left many, if not most, homes hollow shells, void of any resemblance to the family sanctuary of ancient times. An egocentric generation has reduced the home to little more than an overnight rest stop for strangers. The family table (*qua* snack bar or merely refrigerator) has become little more than a feeding station for an increasingly restless generation on the move.

The assertion that every want and whim must be an inalienable right has fertilized the growth of perhaps history's most selfish generation. The "have-it-your-way" mentality has been so reinforced by clever advertising that even a chest-thumping popular song boasts, "I did it my way." Parents are so acclimated to demanding their rights that they give little thought to sacrificing in order to maintain a secure family environment.

This is an institutionally stimulated generation that wants to be free to feel, not to think. Because everything is assigned value on the basis of either feeling or utility, everything is consequently devalued. The music industry has become a diabolical medium for disseminating hate, violence, promiscuity, and perversion. The more vile the performance, the more admired and imitated the idol. The result is that in much of Western society today alley-cat morality is glamorized, and canine mores are the norm. Children of the MTV generation are governed by one rule, "What's in it for me?", and dominated by one maxim, "If it feels good, do it." The quest of the masses is for *joie de vivre* in unbridled and unending excess.

In this "enlightened" age of personal freedoms, absolute ethics and demands for standards of conduct are old-hat: they are antiquated relics of man's past ignorance and superstition. Religions that make demands are enemies of progress and must be stamped out. The only absolute that absolutely exists in this generation is the understanding that there are absolutely no absolutes. Any restrictions on individual "liberties" must be dealt with in harsh, restrictive ways.

Because of this mentality, everything has been redefined. Even history has been rewritten by revisionists with an agenda of pluralism that includes every position except the absolutist and particularist views of monotheistic faith. Marriage is being redefined, not in biblical terms but in aberrant ones to promote politically correct agendas. Family is being so violently restructured that the "nuclear family" of husband, wife, and children is increasingly threatened with extinction.

In Europe, neo-paganism and secularism have conspired to overwhelm Christianity, giving rise to a generation that knows no God and lacks even basic morality. In Germany ancient Teutonic gods are openly worshipped with fertility exercises that would have made the ancient Greeks and Babylonians blush. France has been described as a perfect example of what a nation can become when it is wholly without God. Britain is but a shell of its former self with the current king-in-waiting expecting his oath of office to include a politically correct commitment to defend all religions, not just the biblical faith to which his ancestors swore fealty.

In much of the former Soviet Union, social experimentation and brainwashing began at tender ages when children were taken from parents and educated by the state, becoming, in effect, state children. In a homogenized society, all homes were the same. They served only as vehicles for the state religion, atheism. The result of this social experimentation is that nations with malfunctioning moral compasses now find it necessary to invite Western Christians to teach ethics in schools and colleges just to maintain some semblance of civil order.

Likewise, in China the Chairman-Mao brand of communism has made everyone property of the state and legalized forced abortions for anyone who dared to threaten the well being of the state by having more than one child. This utilitarian view has made the masses expendable, including Christians who survive only as an underground church.

Even in nations that were once profoundly clannish and family-centered, the madness of family-bashing has diminished formerly strong family ties. Values that had endured for millennia have been cast to the wind in an all-consuming quest for a homogenized, politically correct world society. Whole nations are being pressured to redefine both marriage and family in categories that are inimical to the health of individuals, children, and society itself–all in the name of "tolerance." The truth is that everything is to be tolerated except those religions that make demands with required absolutes–Judaism and Christianity. These enemies of individual "freedom" must eventually be entirely eradicated.

COLD HEART, WARM HEART?

Jesus made this observation about the age of lawlessness: "Because of the increase of wickedness, the love of most will grow cold."[2] Herein is the root cause of the unrelenting attacks on the institution of the family and home. Evil triumphs because men of conscience say little or nothing. As lawlessness, even hatred of God's laws, becomes more abundant, the love that is the essence of the Divine diminishes in human hearts to be replaced by an insatiable desire for self-fulfillment and pleasure. The world which once featured much humanitarianism and concern for the downtrodden is ruled by those who think of nothing except self. When men's concerns are only for themselves, there is no depth to which they will not stoop. When men are wrapped up in themselves, they become smaller and smaller packages.

Because of sin, the world has become an increasingly cold and cruel place. The very sanctity of the home has been invaded by these sinister forces, making a growing percentage of homes dark, loveless places. Society's heart has been blackened by sin, and love has been crowded out, replaced by self interest and diverse perversions. Then society weeps over kids killing kids in schools. Weapons, poverty, and political oppression are blamed–anything except the sin that is the real cause of this manifest evil.

Even though iniquity abounds, there is one positive assurance from God's Word: "Where sin increased, grace abounded all the more."[3] God's grace is always superabundant, more than enough to meet every challenge. It is time for the fire of God's presence to warm the heart of a cold world. It is time that a renewal movement sweep over the societies of men throughout the world to restore the biblical models for home and family.

With the profound level of disrespect for authority and the lack of civility and etiquette in large segments of society, particularly in the younger generation, a restoration of biblical models for the home is not only a growing need in society but is also an indispensable requisite for its continued existence. If Western society is to survive the challenges of neo-paganism, monism, and secularism, a "back-to-the-Bible" movement must begin at the most fundamental level of society and the church, the family.

Societal renewal begins and continues one family at a time. The nations of the world do not need simply a multi-splendorous manifestation of ecclesiastical triumphalism. They need to be rebuilt from the foundation up. Restoring the family sanctuary is society's first and foremost need. The world needs millions of Joshuas who will make the resounding proclamation: "As for me and my house, we will serve the Lord."[4] Rather than worrying about the rest of society and seeking to devise strategies to demand societal compliance with biblical morality, leaders are better served by conforming their lives and those of their own families to the mores of God's Word.

Morality can never be legislated. It is a heart issue. Only changed hearts can conform to the image of God's Son,[5] by "keeping his commandments."[6] Church and societal leaders should fulfill to the best of their ability their public functions, but they must be as King David, who was focused on "blessing his household" even after leading Israel in one of the most ecstatic exercises of worship in recorded history.[7]

To effect change in society and the world, those who are passionate for God's kingdom must begin with society's heart and soul, their own homes. To rebuild battered and ruined cities and nations, each family must restore godliness to itself first. A workable strategy for world renewal and restoration to biblical morality is that which Nehemiah used to rebuild the ruined city of Jerusalem: every family worked on the part of the wall in front of its house.[8] When believing families restore the biblical home, the inevitable impact will begin to multiply and resound around the globe.

Grace can abound, love can be renewed, and the family sanctuary can be restored. The biblical ideal can emerge when God's family returns to his guidebook for successful living, the Bible. God can and will create in society a clean heart,[9] but he will do it one family at a time. The coming renewal that will sweep across the world will take place only in the context of the family sanctuary.

[1] Wyatt M. Rogers, Jr. *Christianity and Womanhood* (Westport, Connecticut: Praeger Press, 2002), p. 25.

[2] Matthew 24:12, New International Version.

[3] Romans 5:20, New American Standard Bible (1995).

[4] Joshua 24:15.

[5] Romans 8:29.

[6] John 14:15.

[7] 2 Samuel 6:20.

[8] Nehemiah 3:23-28

[9] Psalm 51:10.

Chapter 2

Paradise: The Prototype

Finding Heaven on Earth

The pattern for the family and home was first established in heaven itself. In reality, the fundamental earthly social unit was functionally in place in the heavenly realm before the terrestrial creation was summoned into existence by the divine Word.[1] The material creation was merely a manifestation of the pattern in the heavenlies.[2] God's will on earth was first revealed in heaven.[3]

In biblically Hebraic tradition, God is clearly identified as the Heavenly Father, not merely the force of nature that many other religions and philosophies espouse. In the "Lord's Prayer," Jesus' précis of long-standing Jewish prayer tradition, Christian disciples are instructed to address God, not as Creator of the universe, but as "our Father."[4] The God of the Bible is God in relation to his family. Called in Jewish tradition *Avinu, Malkenu* (our Father, our King), God is first father of his children and then sovereign of the universe. He is not just the father of humanity's progenitor, Adam;[5] he is the God of Abraham, the God of Isaac, the God of Jacob, and the God and Father of all.[6] Even the angelic hosts of heaven are called his children.[7] He is not, therefore, a static God but an active presence, a God and Father of the living. The very definition of divine function, therefore, is the Father of his children.

While the predominant metaphorical image of God is that of father,[8] heaven is not, however, exclusively masculine. The Jewish apostle to the nations declared that heavenly Jerusalem is the "mother of us all."[9] The prototype for the earthly Jerusalem (both the literal city and the spiritual city) has a maternal image toward humankind. The angelic hosts of heaven hover in a "motherly manner" over the terrestrial creation. It is a simple biblical truth that every believer, indeed every human being, has a guardian angel who always beholds the Father's face, something that humans are not permitted to do.[10] Angels are given charge over each individual child of God,[11] an assignment that conveys to them a maternal relationship to the believer. Jewish *aggadot* suggest that each believer has four guardian angels, one in front, one behind, and one on each side of himself. The corporate heavenly Jerusalem is the mother of the corporate community of terrestrial believers, the Jerusalem that comes down to earth, metaphorically the Messiah's bride.[12]

Humankind shares to a lesser degree and in a lesser dimension[13] the imbued spark of the divine with which the heavenly creation is infused. When God himself breathed into Adam the breath of life,[14] he deposited in him a measure of the living Word of God[15] that has caused divine instructions to be impressed upon his and every subsequent human heart.[16] The human conscience is the manifestation of God's character that was God-breathed into humankind and remains a spark of the divine in each human life. The entire human family bears the spiritual image and likeness of its Creator and Father.

God's children, therefore, are part of a heavenly nuclear family. It should come as no surprise that the heavenly familial pattern was replicated in the earthly family. Heaven came to earth when God formed the first human family in Eden, establishing on planet earth a family sanctuary.

THE EDENIC IDEAL

One need only look at the record of humanity's creation to understand the value that God placed on the family and the home from time immemorial. After God had completed the creation of the inanimate universe, he turned his focus to the earth, the place where he would deposit life in millions of living organisms. After the myriads of species of plants and animals were in place, God's final creative impulse was to form his crowning creation, the being in which he would manifest his own image and likeness.[17] He then formed mankind, humanity personified in one human being.

From the moment that God gathered together a clump of dust from the earth and began to shape it, all the genetic coding that would be required for the entire human race was present. The being that God created was called The Adam (הָאָדָם, *ha-Adam*). This being is the only person in all of Holy Scripture whose name is prefixed by the definite article.[18] This was not *Adam*, a solitary male being, but *ha-Adam*, The Adam or humanity. In reality, *ha-Adam* was the identity that described the essence of all humanity: "The Dirt Being." *Adam* derives from *adamah*, which means dirt or earth. *Ha-Adam* was formed from *ha-adamah*, the human from the humus, the earthling from the earth.

After God had assembled the correct proportions of terrestrial dust, he structured the first being of humanity and vivified that lifeless form with his divine breath, the breath of life. More than the *nefesh* (soul) that he shared with all the animal creation, Adam was a *living* soul, infused with the divine breath of life (*neshamah*).

At the very moment of this being's creation, The Adam was both male and female. "God created man in his own image . . . male and female created he *them*" (emphasis added).[19] A subsequent recapitulation of this divine creative moment makes this declaration: "Male and female created he them; and blessed them, and called *their* name [שְׁמָם] Adam [הָאָדָם], in the day that *they* were created"[20] (emphasis added). From the moment of humanity's creation, the name given to this entity was *ha-Adam*. They, both male and female, were called The Adam. The newly formed being was not the genderless androgyne of mythology. It was also not simply a male creation. It was humanity. All the genetic material necessary for gender-specific existence was present in the human body from the moment God formed it from the dust of the earth.

FOUNDATION OF FAMILY

The formation of "woman" was not a divine afterthought when the omniscient God suddenly came to realize that his new male creation lacked companionship. Nor was woman's creation God's effort to rectify a divine mistake by forming a secondary and inferior servant gender from masculine spare parts. The formation of Eve represented the separation from The Adam of that part of humanity that was feminine and the formation of a body and spirit entity that was complementary in every way to the masculine remnant of original humanity. The only difference between the now two beings was their gender: Adam was אִישׁ (*ish*); Eve was אִשָּׁה (*ishah*, the feminine form of *ish*). Both were still *ha-Adam*, humanity. This was the edenic foundation of family.

After *ha-Adam* was anesthetized, divine surgery removed from the being an anatomical part that has been universally defined as a "rib." The word in Hebrew is צֵלָע (*tzela*), which elsewhere in Scripture is translated "side,"[21] "chamber,"[22] "beam,"[23] "brow (of a hill),[24] or "to limp or stumble."[25] Only in the human creation narrative is the word *tzela* rendered "rib." From this statement, some theologians have even suggested (with amazing anatomical inaccuracy!)

that men have one less rib than women, and others have extrapolated the preposterous idea that "feminine guile" is the result of woman's creation from a "crooked bone." This idea has reinforced the perception that femininity is inferior to masculinity, as though the male Adam had a superfluous anatomical part that God used to create an assistant to a superior creation.

The translation of *tzela* as "rib" is possible because of the word's etymological connection with the arched beams of the temple or with the brow (rib) of a hill. Indeed, *tzela* was and remains the Hebrew word for "rib." If such were the case, The Adam either had an extra rib before the surgery or afterwards had a deficiency that was not transmitted to subsequent male progeny. On the other hand, *tzela* could speak figuratively or could even be translated "chamber" as a euphemism for uterus ("arched side chamber") and related organs that would have been a logical basis for the formation of the first female being. Whatever the case, all of the genetic material necessary for woman was present in the side of The Adam from the moment of human creation, and its removal left a void that God "closed up with flesh."[26]

The narrative of Eve's formation is interesting in that it declares that "God made an *ishah* [woman] from the *tzela* [rib or side chamber] he had taken out of *ha-Adam* [mankind]."[27] When God brought the woman to Adam, he observed, "This is now at last bone of my bone and flesh of my flesh," and he named her, "*ishah* [woman], because she was taken out of *ish* [man]."[28] The divine narrative declares that the woman was taken from mankind (*ha-Adam*), while the remaining masculine being recognized his new companion as having been taken from man (*ish*), or from himself. The now masculine Adam realized right away that what was standing before him was genuinely a part of himself, not some other substance or inferior creation, but a being equally human, complementary in every way to himself.

Before God separated Eve from The Adam, he had

brought before the human entity all the animal creation so that The Adam could name each of them. It then became clear to the human that none of these beings was comparable to mankind. God also observed that it was not good for mankind to exist as a solitary being. Whereas his entire creation had been "good" and even "very good," for the first time, something was lacking: the absence of suitable companionship for God's crowning creation was "not good."

God, therefore, separated the feminine gender of mankind from its masculine gender. The result was man and woman (*ish* and *ishah*)–separate, but equal beings with complementary genders. This is why when Adam first saw Eve, he exclaimed, "At last!" After viewing and naming all the other animal creation, he could without hesitation recognize that this creature was from, of, and for him. It was like seeing the essence of his own being flashed before him in a mirror, all personified in Eve! Here was his true alter-ego.

The separation of the *tzela* and the subsequent formation of Eve in no way weakened Adam. The fact that woman was formed around something that was described as a "chamber" similar to those side chambers in Solomon's temple should suggest that the woman brought a unique strength to the new human family. Just as the arch is one of the strongest of architectural structures, so woman has always had an inner strength that has brought help to man and has strengthened him for the role that God has determined for him.

Just as God had not been content to dwell in isolation but had created the hosts of heaven, so it was not good for The Adam to remain alone. Humanity is by design a gregarious creation. The reclusive ascetic is the exception to the rule. Withdrawal from social interaction is aberrant behavior, contrary to divine intent and divine instruction. Even celibacy is not the biblical norm.[29] God's very first commandments to mankind were to "be fruitful and multiply and fill the earth,"[30] and those commandments have never been abrogated. Each human being fully realizes his humanity and his God-given potential, therefore, in the context of marriage and family.

COMPLEMENTARY COMPANIONSHIP

The sole purpose for the separation of human genders, then, was the creation of interpersonal relationship, a sublime fellowship of mutual affirmation and counterbalance. The separation of the one humanity into two human beings was the cure for loneliness. From the beginning of human generation, therefore, God's design was for companionship and communion of complementary beings.

The basis for the common unity of community was established in the divine intention in separating Eve from Adam. The surgery was not for the purpose of creating division; it was designed to produce a multifaceted unity. When God observed that it was not good for humanity to be alone, he purposed to create a "suitable helper" for him.[31] The Hebrew term **עֵזֶר כְּנֶגְדּוֹ** (*ezer k'negdo*) has been translated "help meet" (qualified helper), which has morphed into the term *helpmate* in English. The inadequate understanding of the Hebrew has given rise to implied scriptural inferiority for the second human being.

Ezer k'negdo, however, in no way implies inferiority in Hebrew. *Ezer* is the same word that teaches that God is man's help. "The LORD . . . is our help [*ezer*] and our shield."[32] Certainly there is no thought of inferiority in God the *ezer* (helper) of mankind! Why, then, should inferiority be ascribed to woman as man's *ezer*? In reality, the context of the feminine formation narrative implies the truth. God purposed to create a power comparable or equal to Adam and in order to do so, separated a part of The Adam and around it formed Eve. The woman was neither inferior nor superior to the man. She was a means of security and solidarity, a help and shield.

Eve was Adam's complement, bringing inner strength, wisdom, and insight to their joint life. Because she was made of something from inside Adam, she was gifted with intuition, the ability to see through facades into the innermost motives and to discern with visceral feeling, not rationalization or analysis.[33] In order for Adam to have these insights, he needed a "help," his wife. Likewise, Eve lacked a part of what was left in Adam and consequently has an innate desire toward her husband to resort to the elements of strength, drive, and provision that he brings to the superentity of two-in-one. Theirs was to be more than a partnership, it was to be a covenantal relationship in which both counterbalanced and complemented the other.

This truth is further established in the second part of the appellative for woman, *ezer k'negdo*. The phrase *k'negdo* means "over against" or "in front of." The implication in the "help-meet" passage is that Eve is "equal to or adequate to" Adam. While the phrase can also mean "in opposition to," it is clear from the context that it implies a qualified, equal power who brought a measure of strength to the human interpersonal relationship that the man could not offer. Eve was to be a counterbalance to Adam, elevating the quality of their relationship and reinforcing their unity by adding what her husband lacked.

The phrase *in front of* also implies the unique relationship that Adam and Eve and their subsequent counterparts of masculine and feminine humanity would enjoy above all others. They were to have a "face-to-face" relationship of mutual respect and affirmation toward one another, a relationship akin to the *panim el-panim* (face-to-face) intimacy that Adam and Eve had with God in the Garden.[34] From Eden onward, the foundation of the human family would be the open and unashamed relationship between one man and one woman. The woman was not to be in a subservient position several paces behind the man. She was to be in front of him, facing him, exchanging mutually affirming love with him. They were to be on the same level, equal beings with different physical and emotional characteristics.

Even the physical intimacy experienced in the human

family was a manifestation of the one-to-one, face-to-face relationship of equality and openness. As they fulfilled God's first commandment to "be fruitful and multiply," Adam and Eve became "one flesh." What God had joined together in covenant was now intertwined in loving conjugation. Unlike the rest of the animal creation, the human couple shared their intimacy in a face-to-face, mouth-to-mouth embrace. Their anatomy was so designed that especially in their most passionate moment, they were *panim el-panim*, complementary equals facing and embracing each other.

The manifestation of the female was also for the purpose of complementing the male, not for canceling or opposing him. Femininity is a counterbalance to masculinity. When mankind became two, both halves were necessary for optimum efficiency in the human family. Without the woman, man would be eccentric, out of balance. Likewise, without the man, the woman would be discordant, lacking equanimity. For this reason alone, men and women were never designed to be identical. They have always possessed different, yet complementary characteristics. They fulfill different, yet mutually reciprocal roles. Modern society's insistence upon a politically correct "unisex" view of men and women is an affront to both God and nature. If male and female were identical, one would be superfluous. God would never have made two if one were adequate.

It is for this reason that Judaism has long taught that every human being has another half. It is foundational not only to the ongoing survival of the human species but also to the health of the human family that men and women find and be reconnected with their other half. Celibacy is, therefore, not a viable option for either man or woman from a purely Hebraic standpoint. It is God's design that the two be made one as was demonstrated in the Edenic ideal. Two males or two females cannot be complete together, for both male and female are required to form the superentity of oneness that is complete. Male and female in and of themselves are complete personalities, but marriage brings together these complete persons into a new and unique completeness of fulfilling relationship. What the husband lacks, the wife adds. What the wife needs, the husband provides.

TWO BEINGS, ONE FAMILY

The restoration of the original oneness of humanity by bringing together a man and a woman was not solely for the perpetuation of the species. The fact that man and woman can be joined anatomically into oneness is a by-product of the oneness that God designed for the human family. Oneness is first a spiritual unity achieved through divinely commissioned agreement. The covenant of marriage involves three persons–man, woman, and God–and it was designed from the beginning to be indissoluble.[35] This kind of relationship creates the strongest of geometric structures, with God at the top of the triangle and man and woman on an equal plane at the bottom. Some Jewish scholars have suggested that even in marital conjugation, three persons are involved: husband, wife, and God.

The unity that creates a family is not a state of uniformity, a unisex state of sameness where a blurring of identities and roles dominates and confuses. It is a state of pluriformity, a unity in diversity that is manifest in cohesion. This is the biblical definition of unity. It is the state of being *echad* (one), a oneness similar in nature to the oneness of God himself, who is also declared to be one in the fundamental statement of Jewish and

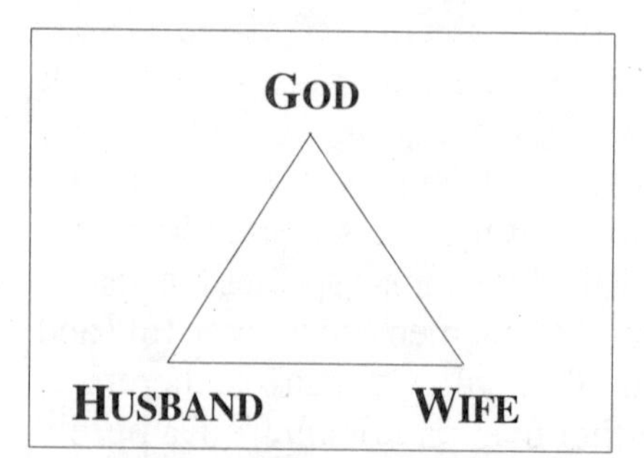

The strongest geometric structure is a triangle. Likewise, the family is at its strongest when husband and wife are totally committed and submitted to each another in covenant equality and are mutually submitted to God.

Christian faith, the *Shema*: "Hear, O Israel, the Lord our God is one [*echad*] Lord."[36]

The reunification of man and woman, then, was the immediate divine instruction after mankind's gender separation. "Hence a man leaves his father and mother and clings to his wife, so that they become one flesh."[37] The Authorized Version is more memorable, declaring that man is to "leave" and "cleave"–leave his parents and cleave to his wife so that they subsequently become "one flesh." From the formation of the very first family in Eden, it has been clear that the social order for the human creation would be this: man and woman would leave their paternal and maternal relationships to form a new entity replicating that first social unit–one man and one woman joined together in a oneness of ultimate unity. Sexual relations merely demonstrates physically what has already been accomplished spiritually by divine covenant. Two have become one.

Marriage was designed to be the cement that joins the fundamental societal unit in an ever-strengthening bond. Indeed, what God has joined together, man is not to put asunder.[38] Husband and wife were to be "glued together," as the Hebrew word דָּבַק (*dabak*) that is generally translated "join" or "cleave" is more accurately rendered. Marriage was not to be a casual, intermittent relationship based solely on emotional or hormonal responses. It was to be a life-long covenantal relationship that would provide a secure, stable environment for the nurturing of children and the perpetuation of the human family. It represented a divine bonding that created a unity, a superentity that was greater than its constituent parts.

Adam and Eve not only fit together anatomically, they were suited to one another in every way. They were the full realization of total humanity in male and female returned to unity. They complemented one another. They were perfect counterparts. They fit together emotionally, intellectually, spiritually. Everything that one needed was found in the other. As they were cemented in indissoluble unity, neither had any lack. Their oneness was the perfect state for adding to the human family the children that God purposed for them. Though sin entered in and brought dysfunctionality to the family of humanity, God's intention was clear. The human family was patterned after the heavenly design. God's tabernacle was with humanity.

The human family, therefore, has always been and will always be defined by its most fundamental unit, the nuclear family. What God originally instituted in Eden was to be the pattern for all subsequent ideal manifestations of humanity. The institution of the family was to be foundational for the social interaction of all humankind. Only when the sanctity of the home is upheld is a basis established for security and growth both in the church and in society.

HEAVEN ON EARTH

The quality of the divine relationship between the heavenly Father and the heavenly Jerusalem was the pattern for the Edenic family. The original center for social and spiritual development was the garden home. Loving, affirming relationships made the home a true sanctuary. There was no temple, no tabernacle, not even a chapel. Every social interaction and every act of worship was done solely in the context of the family. The home was the true sanctuary.

Since the time when God created the first family, that pattern has been replicated generation after generation as humans leave, cleave, and multiply, fulfilling the divine plan for planet earth. Heaven continues to be manifest on earth in the form of the home. The ideal family is a paradise in itself, a true sanctuary of safety and repose. God's heavenly pattern always works when employed on earth.

The sages of Israel have long viewed God as a matchmaker, insisting that the work in which he has engaged himself since he completed the Genesis creation is the making of marriages and families. It is God's purpose to bring together the separated halves of the human family, the man and woman who are intended for each other. If this is true, marriage is really the proverbial match made in heaven.

The human longing for companionship and the fulfillment of the divine command for marital union is innate in the psyche and in the hormonal chemistry of human existence. God uses what he has formed naturally in humanity to fulfill his purposes in replicating the original family in their garden home, the ever-renewed paradise that God created for humankind, the family sanctuary

[1] Colossians 1:16; John 1:3.
[2] Hebrews 8:5.
[3] Matthew 6:10.
[4] Matthew 6:9.
[5] Luke 3:37.
[6] Matthew 22:32. In defining himself as the God of Abraham, the God of Isaac, and the God of Jacob, the Eternal manifest himself as a God of the living, not of the long-dead. He was not just Adam's Father; he is the Father of all.
[7] Job 1:6; 38:7.
[8] There are various scriptural, metaphorical images that represent God as having a feminine and maternal nature (e.g., the God who is the Creator/Father in Deuteronomy 3:6 is the God who gave birth to Israel in Deuteronomy 3:18). In reality, however, God is genderless Spirit, and the anthropomorphisms that Scripture ascribes to him are material means of communicating understanding about God. Romans 1:20 declares that the invisible God is understood (but never worshipped) through the things that are made.
[9] Galatians 4:26.
[10] Matthew 18:10; 1 Timothy 6:16.
[11] Psalm 91:11.
[12] Revelation 21:9-10.
[13] Psalm 8:5; Hebrews 2:7, 9.
[14] Genesis 2:7
[15] 2 Timothy 3:16. The Holy Scriptures are the God-breathed manifestation 2 Timothy 3:16) of the living Word, the divine *Logos* (John 1:1-4).
[16] Romans 2:15. Man's conscience is a spark of divinity, the imprint of the divine in the form of the foundational commandments for human conduct that are written on all men's hearts.
[17] Genesis 1:26.
[18] Scripture never calls Abraham *ha-Avraham* (the-Abraham) or David *ha-David* (the-David). Adam is called *ha-Adam* because this being was not just a human male, but all of humanity.
[19] Genesis 1:27.

[20] Genesis 5:2.

[21] Exodus 25:12; 26:35; 30:4; Job 18:12; 1 Kings 6:8.

[22] 1 Kings 6:5, 8; Ezekiel 41:5, 9-11, 26.

[23] 1 Kings 6:15.

[24] 2 Samuel 16:3.

[25] Psalm 35:15; 38:17; Micah 4:7; Zephaniah 3:19.

[26] Genesis 2:21, New International Version.

[27] Genesis 2:22, New International Version.

[28] Genesis 2:23, New International Version.

[29] Celibacy has been preferred in times of great persecution (1 Corinthians 7:27) and by those who have made the sacrifice of depriving themselves of companionship in order to advance the kingdom of God (Matthew 19:12). This, however, is a personal choice and never a divine requirement. God's commandment is that human beings should marry and create a family: "Leave father and mother and be joined together . . . be fruitful and multiply and fill the earth." Rabbinic Judaism has insisted that any person who is not married is incomplete and is in violation of the divine commandment to "be fruitful and multiply." In Jewish history, however, there is evidence of sages who were bachelors (at least until later life). Jesus himself was not married even at the age of 33. Additionally, those who were widowed at an early age were often never remarried (cf. Luke 2:36-37, where Anna, the prophetess, who had been widowed only seven years after her wedding, subsequently lived much of her remaining years in the temple and was 84 at the time of Jesus' birth).

[30] Genesis 1:22.

[31] Genesis 2:18.

[32] Psalm 33:20; cf. 115:11, King James Version; cf. Psalm 70:5; 124:8; Hosea 13:9.

[33] Muriel Mohabir, "A Woman Designed by God," in *Sisters with Power*, Joe Eldred, ed. (London: Cortemus, 2000), p. 125.

[34] *Panim el-panim* (פָּנִים אֶל־פָּנִים) is the ideal state of intimacy with God that the righteous achieved in Scripture (cf. Moses in Exodus 33:11).

[35] Though divorce is quite acceptable in Hebraic culture under given sets of circumstances, Jesus made it clear that God's original intent was for marital permanence (cf. Matthew 19:6-8). In verse 9 of this passage Jesus also established the principal legitimate reason for divorce and remarriage as marital infidelity. Paul further approved divorce and remarriage for abandonment, indicating that failure to fulfill the contract of the marriage covenant can result in its being voided (cf. 1 Corinthians 7:15).

[36] Deuteronomy 6:4.

[37] Genesis 2:24, Jewish Publication Society *Tanakh*.

[38] Matthew 19:6.

Chapter 3

The Domestic Temple

CENTER FOR HUMAN DEVELOPMENT

Adam and Eve communed with God when he came to their garden home in the cool of the day.[1] They did not go to a shrine that God had built for them. God came to them in their home, the very first house church. Their home was a natural place for worship and communion. It needed no embellishment or grandiose, imposing façade. Everything was simple. It was just Adam and Eve–the first family–and God. The progenitors of the human race walked with God in a sweet communion of blissful joy and fulfillment.

Even after the fall, the human family was not given a physical sanctuary in which to repose for interaction with God. Indeed, the process continued as the simple act of "walking with God."[2] For those descendants of Adam who remained faithful to God, the Eternal was ever-present, not some distant, unapproachable being or one who could be approached only in the confines of a specific space. The prototype in heaven was replicated in the human family on earth. The heavenly sanctuary, as it were, came down to man and was manifest in the home.

Enoch, the seventh from Adam, was so dedicated to this divine walk that he was translated from earth to God's presence.[3] Subsequently the divine order for family disintegrated when the sons of God were joined to the daughters of men.[4] Finally, only Noah had maintained the purity of his lineage,[5] and as a result he "found grace in the eyes of the LORD"[6] and saved humanity in his family sanctuary, the ark. Salvation from the deluge was accomplished in the context of family. The family, therefore, was the locus for spiritual relationship in the beginning of time, and it remained so in the patriarchal age.

THE ABRAHAMIC FAMILY OF FAITH

Sarah and Abraham's tent was a shining example of the a family sanctuary, a home church. Though theirs was a transient, nomadic existence, they had a fixed and continuing sanctuary, their family. Their tent was their place of meeting, fellowship, study, and prayer. Though Abraham appeared before the priest-king of Salem to make an offering and receive a blessing,[7] his principal venue for interaction with God was his own home, with his own family and the myriads of guests who frequented their portable sanctuary.

Rabbinic tradition asserts that Sarah's tent was open on all four sides, demonstrating the profound hospitality of her home. It also suggests that Sarah was such a powerful prophetess that she is believed to be the first woman to whom the powerful ode of praise recorded in Proverbs 31 was sung. This home was so godly that it could welcome the Lord himself into its fellowship. Accompanied by two angels, God came to the sanctuary of Abraham and Sarah's tent.[8]

Abraham became the father of the faithful because he believed God and immediately carried out his divine instructions.[9] He also ensured the fact that his descendants after him would do justice and love mercy by instructing them in their family sanctuary.[10] Abraham's faithfulness in family worship and teaching gained him the favor of God and was among the divine reasons for his election as the progenitor of the faith race.

Until the time when God brought the Hebrew descendants of the patriarch of faith to Sinai and there constituted them as the nation of Israel, all the worship functions of the Abrahamic family were carried out in the context of the family. Even the great event that brought their freedom from Egyptian slavery was manifest not in a corporate worship experience but in each individual Israelite home.

"Place the lamb's blood on the doorposts and lintels of your houses," the Israelites were instructed. "Remain in your houses, eating the roasted lamb and the bread of haste (*matzoh*)."[11] Surely God could have had Moses instruct Aaron to sacrifice one lamb for all of Israel in a solemn public ceremony. One great liturgical exercise for all would have made more sense! But, the action that brought salvation to Israel was a family affair. Moses had instructed the Israelites: "Each man is to take a lamb for his family, one for each household."[12] God was going to deliver all of Israel; however, the method that he would employ for their deliverance was manifest one family at a time through house-church worship that lasted the entire night!

From the time of the Exodus until the present day, the primary annual worship experience for the descendants of those who were delivered from Egypt has been the Passover. The divine appointment has been celebrated from year to year for millennia in the context of family as it was on that first Passover night. Parents and grandparents lead each family in this act of remembrance that God enjoined that night upon the Israelites throughout all their generations, forever. All family members, from the oldest to the youngest, celebrate the fact that they were personally delivered from Egypt. The entire celebration remains foremost a family worship experience. In the spirit of the hospitality that is so essential to the Jewish mindset, the family sanctuary is also expanded to include extended family members (aunts, uncles, cousins, nephews, and nieces), friends, and even strangers. The family sanctuary is not a closed, exclusive circle. It is an open, inclusive company that invites others to share in the sanctity of familial worship and fellowship.

Following the Exodus, the Hebrew family became God's nation, a kingdom of priests.[13] Assembled at Sinai, all the families of the Israelites were organized into one extended family, the corporate assembly of Israel. The newly birthed nation received a constitution, the Torah, an outline of God's instructions to his children. Within that constitution were instructions of how the unified family of Israel as a corporate entity should worship in covenant with God. In effect, the thousands of home churches in the Sinai desert became history's largest mega-church, one of perhaps two million people! Corporate and community fellowship, study, and worship are essential and can be of any size that is practical; however, the fundamental unit of every corporate body must always be the family.

GOD'S TENT–MAN'S TENT

In order to facilitate corporate worship and to systematize and standardize a uniform order for personal and family devotion, God instructed Moses to build a sanctuary, a *mishkan* (tabernacle). The sanctuary was to be portable, housed in a tent. God's sanctuary was to go with the people, not vice versa.[14] The central elements of that material structure were transportable, designed to accompany the Israelites wherever they went. God's house had no fixed dwelling place. It was simply with his people. Just as God had maintained personal contact with the foundational entity of his society, the home, so the tabernacle in the wilderness was established to function in the midst of the camp of Israel: God's tent was right in the middle of all the family tents of this transient people.

The implements and appliances of God's house were not mystifying objects that were beyond understanding of all but a monastic, priestly class. They were objects that reflected ordinary Hebrew family values. The laver that demanded ritual purity of the priests and the sacrifices was but a formal manifestation of the Israelites' concern with personal cleanliness. "Change your garments and be clean," their father Jacob had already commanded them after his encounter with God at Peniel.[15] The table of shewbread merely underscored their understanding that God was the one who brought forth bread from the earth and rained down bread from heaven for their sustenance in the desert.[16] The menorah reflected the light that had symbolized the divine presence in their homes long before it did so in the sanctuary. The altar of incense reflected their love of spices and the smells of sweetness in contrast to the malodorous scents of life among the various animals that were essential to their nomadic existence. The portable sanctuary, therefore, was patterned after the Israelite tent home, dating back to Sarah and Abraham's tent and beyond.

After Israel inherited the Promised Land, the focus of worship remained with the family. The primary vehicle for social and worship activities was the home. No greater illustration of this truth can be found than in the narrative one of Israel's most exhilarating corporate worship exercises. When King David returned the Ark of the Covenant to prominence in Israel, he led the assembled multitude in ecstatic praise, dancing before the Lord with all his might. What a profound public demonstration of passionate devotion to the God of Israel! David's thoughts, however, were not lost in this profound exercise of public worship, a momentary existential experience. He immediately retired to his home for this express purpose: "David returned to bless his household."[17]

Even though there were priests in Israel who had been

specifically commissioned with the responsibility of bestowing God's blessing on the children of Israel,[18] David remembered his primary role as the leader of his household and returned from a great corporate worship exercise to the sanctuary of his home so he could bless his family. David's home, not the congregation or its establishment for religion, was his primary sanctuary of blessing and the place for his personal devotion.

Subsequently, David wanted what he had in the splendor of his palace to be replicated and even superseded in a national sanctuary for all Israel.[19] He purposed to build God a house. God did not specifically give instructions for this structure as he had for the tabernacle; however, he allowed Solomon to complete the task. At that time, the official religion was established in the temple.

THE MINI-TEMPLE

After many generations, the political leadership and the temple cultus became so corrupt and oppressive that God himself summoned a pagan king to destroy both. Nebuchadnezzar the Babylonian overwhelmed Jerusalem, destroyed the palaces and the temple, and led the people away in chains of captivity. Faced with the loss of the very implements and system of worship that they had come to trust, the Israelites were challenged to find an alternate means of worshipping God. By the rivers of Babylon, they hung their harps on the willows and lamented, "How can we sing the LORD's songs in a foreign land?"[20]

Their grief over the loss of their corporate sanctuary could not, however, suppress their passion for worshipping God. After a time, they recognized that God could again be worshipped in the context of their own homes and in corporate exercises in the same ways in which he had been honored before either the tabernacle or the temple had been built. They came to realize that the center of worship had always been the home and that the corporate exercises of worship to which they were called[21] could be fulfilled outside the temple cultus. What eventually became formalized in their understanding and belief was first a practical reality in their lives. Their homes became mini-temples. Then, as families assembled for fellowship and corporate worship, their meetings became mini-temples.

In the exile, the emphasis of worship was returned to the people, to the family, and to the extended family, the synagogue. There was no temple, no formal material structures dedicated exclusively to worship. The synagogues were meetings (reunions), and the synagogues assembled in homes or in public places. The family was the church, and the church was the extended family, the congregation.[22] Buildings were not the object of worship: God was! And God could be worshipped in the most humble of sanctuaries, even in the hovel of a slave family's hut.

When Israel returned from captivity to rebuild Jerusalem and the temple, the newly discovered (perhaps even newly restored) institution of the synagogue continued. Worship could be maintained even without a central geographical focus. It could be manifest in each meeting of the people, whether just a single family assembled for study and devotion or in a meeting of hundreds or thousands of extended family members (the synagogue).

Eventually, the sages of Israel came to view each Jewish home as a *mikdash me'at*, a small sanctuary or mini-temple. As such, the home was viewed as a small version of the ancient temple in Jerusalem. What had functioned for millennia without formalization was finally recognized by Israel's spiritual leaders. The Jewish home remains to this day a mini-sanctuary. The one institution that God designed as foundational for relationship among his earthly children is to be replicated in each individual home around the world. In reality, the tabernacle and temple were merely extended manifestations of the home. The undeniable importance of the home as the center for spiritual development is clearly underscored by its formal recognition in the Jewish community as a temple in miniature.

A DOMESTIC PRIESTHOOD

In order to carry out the functions of sanctuary, some form of priesthood must be manifest. In Israel's sanctuaries, God ordained the tribe of Levi and more specifically the sons of Aaron to fulfill this role. The functions of the priesthood were threefold: to make sacrifices for sin, to teach God's Word, and to lead in corporate worship. Each of these functions remained fully operative when the first-century New Covenant community emerged.

First, Jesus himself entered into the Most Holy Place in heaven once and for all time, offering his own blood to atone for all the sins of humanity, past, present, and future.[23] Though all will not believe and will not, therefore, be saved from their sins, provision was made in that one event of redemption to atone for all human sin. For the church, the sacrificial role of priesthood under the Sinai covenant was reversed. Whereas the Aaronic priesthood had offered men's sacrifices for sin to God, the priesthood of all believers in the church offers Jesus, God's only sacrifice for sin, to men, saying, "Be reconciled to God."[24] By being the witnesses that he commissioned them to be,[25] this royal priesthood literally sacrifices the gospel of God, offering it to humanity.[26]

Second, the leaders both of the community and the family were commissioned to teach the Word of God. They underscored God's instructions for mankind by both being living witnesses, fulfilling those instructions in their own lives, and by continually reinforcing the responsibility of individuals and the community of faith to be obedient to the law of Christ.

Third, the Christian leaders and heads of household were to lead in acts of worship and praise to the Almighty. All believers everywhere are to do all that they do to the glory of God,[27] to offer sacrifices of praise and thanksgiving to his name,[28] and to ascribe greatness and honor to the Most High God. When a truly Hebraic understanding of worship is present in the church, the exercise of reverence both in congregational and familial settings is continual.[29]

In the New Covenant community, the three functions of priesthood are carried out on four levels. First is the High Priest, Jesus, who atones for sins, teaches righteousness, and engenders worship. Jesus is the High Priest in the temple or sanctuary in heaven.[30] The second level of priesthood is manifest in the leaders whom God has positioned to provide oversight and protection for the community of faith in all of its various levels of manifestation. These are the leaders or priests in the spiritual temple,[31] the congregation. The third level is the priesthood in the home, with the head of each household charged with the responsibility of instructing the family in ways of righteousness and leading in worship. Parents are leaders or priests in the temple of the home. The fourth level is the priesthood of all human beings and more particularly of all believers. Since every human body is designed to be a temple for God,[32] anyone can function as a priest to approach God for himself to obtain the forgiveness of sins and acceptance into the family of God. The only mediator is the High Priest himself.[33] Likewise, all believers who have come to faith in God function as priests on a continuing basis,[34] having direct access to the High Priest for the forgiveness of sins, for understanding of God's instructions for mankind, and for direct worship of the Heavenly Father.

In Christian history, it is the third level of priesthood that has been generally neglected. This is the area that demands restoration for the health of the church in general and for the well-being of individuals in specific. The church has been very careful to give preeminence in all things to Jesus the High Priest. A proper understanding that priesthood extends to all believers has also been prominent in much of Christianity. Additionally, Christians have generally manifest a biblically mandated show of respect for leaders in the church who have been chosen to lead the faith community in things pertaining to God. In the process, however, the organized church and virtually all believers have neglected the important level of priesthood that should function in every home.

It is a simple fact of history that familial worship predated corporate worship, not vice versa. As a matter of fact, corporate exercises were merely extensions of familial worship to the extended family and community. This in no way obviates or minimizes the importance of or the need for organized approaches to corporate worship. It does underscore a long-neglected vital element in the life of the corporate worshipping community that Christians call church. The biblical family was and always will be the locus for spiritual growth. If the family is first a mini-temple, then the congregation is a mini-temple in the expanded dimension for which it was designed.

If the home is a temple, then it follows that a priesthood must be represented in the home. A temple without a functioning priestly office and ritual is nothing but an empty shell, for the sole reason that a temple exists is to facilitate the worship exercises that pertain to the physical structure.

In order to make a home a temple with a functioning priestly office, however, one must have a clear understanding of the principles and practice of priesthood. All the functions of the priesthood in the ancient temple in Jerusalem, therefore, must also be manifest in the home as they are in the corporate community of believers. The form and detail may be somewhat different, but the principles must be faithfully replicated.

The head of each household–ideally the father–should function in a priestly role toward the rest of the family. The firstborn sons of ancient Israel belonged to the Lord. Apparently, God intended that they would make up the priesthood; however, they were redeemed and replaced by the Levites.[35] Since leadership in the home has been biblically delegated to husband and father, he should assume the responsibility of leading his family in things pertaining to God. The ideal, however, is not always the real, for human weakness and sin militate against the ideal. In situations of human brokenness, substitute means are demanded.

Because the church has removed priesthood functions from the home, it has largely emasculated its male members. The church has relegated most of the males in society to a position of being engaged in "secular" work and therefore not doing God's work. For this reason, most males do not see a role for themselves in the church. Christianity has come to recognize as "men of God" only those who are fulfilling roles of public ministry. The rest of men are seen as laborers whose function it is to support their families and the organized church.

The truth is that all men who are believers are "men of God," sharing equally with the "men of the cloth" this title and function. Work itself is worship, and there is no dichotomy between spiritual work and secular work. It is all spiritual, for it fulfills the divine command, "Six days shall you work."[36] It should come as no surprise, therefore, that one of the words for worship in Hebrew is also the word for work: עֲבֹדָה (*abodah*). The church desperately needs to close the centuries-old clergy-laity gap by understanding that all of its members are men and women of God, not just those who are employed professionally by the church. It also needs to restore the biblically Hebraic understanding that husbands and fathers have a God-given responsibility to be "men of God" in their own homes, leading their families in things pertaining to God.

Every man's work must also be understood from a biblical perspective as being a "ministry." The work of ministry is not the exclusive province of those who are gifted to lead the corporate community of believers. It is a function of every man and every woman. The "ministry" of work in every man's life must, however, be emphasized because work was assigned to the man after the fall of Adam and remains man's chief source of self-worth.

When all Christian men come to understand that their work is God's work and that it is a ministry, they are elevated to a state of equality with those men who are leaders in the church. There are no longer two tiers of manhood and worth, clergy and laity. There are simply different functions, different gifts, different administrations. Whereas some are gifted to teach, preach, counsel, or lead in worship, all are gifted with the ministry of working to provide for themselves and their families.

When all work is seen as worship and a ministry, all men can emerge from church-inflicted emasculation to assume the roles of leadership to which they were ordained. Since they are doing God's work throughout the day, they can come to their homes and continue God's work as priestly leaders of their own families. Wives and children can find in their own homes the righteous man who demonstrates all the characteristics of Psalm 1 and Psalm 112. Families can delight in the priestly leadership of their head of household rather than reserving respect and awe for "the Reverend." Much of the counseling load of the clergy would simply disappear.

Men who have recovered this accurate biblical and Hebraic understanding of their own roles do not have to dominate their wives and children in abusive codependencies in order to gain the respect they feel they need. They realize that they are men of God, responsible to exhibit the qualities of love and tender mercy that Christ manifests toward his bride, the church, and that God himself continually extends toward all his children. Assuming the role of priest in the home places an awesome responsibility on a husband and father. He cannot be a dictator with everyone serving his whims. He must be a facilitator, in love serving both his wife and his children and setting an example of right and generous conduct that those little ones who will replace him on earth can follow. He must sacrifice his own ambitions and "needs" for the sake of love for his family in the same manner in which Jesus gave his life out of love for the church.

A HOME CHURCH

Original Christianity was simply an extension and full manifestation of the model of community interaction, study, and worship that had developed during the Babylonian exile and had become normative for the society into which Jesus and the apostles were born. The synagogue (meeting or assembly) was the dominant functioning expression of daily and weekly exercises of worship throughout Israel and the Jewish diaspora in the first century. The synagogues were not buildings; they were meetings of people. Judaism adopted the Greek word συναγωγή (*sunagoge*) meaning "meeting or assembly," to describe this phenomenon.

Though the temple and its priesthood maintained an important role in their lives, the temple cultus had come increasingly to share roles of worship with the synagogue in the everyday lives of the Jewish community of Jesus. It was in this matrix that Jesus and his apostles lived their lives as part of a dynamic Jewish community. It was in this setting that they worshipped and expressed their devotion to God.

The Jewish people had discovered during the Babylonian captivity that they could worship God without the temple and without a functioning priesthood. When Nebuchadnezzar destroyed the temple, the people simply reverted to the worship that had originally been in the homes and extended families before the introduction of the priesthood and its attendant cultus. Meetings sprang up in Jewish communities in the captivity as dutiful, worshipping Jewish families cried out to express public devotion to their God. The foundation of a tradition that has transcended more than two millennia emerged. The synagogue was born.

The earliest synagogues were simply extensions into community-wide models of family worship exercises. First the Jews worshipped God as families; then families came together in communities to worship corporately, thereby multiplying the worship dynamic. The synagogue was never the model that was then replicated in the home. The domestic meeting was rather duplicated and expanded in the synagogue. As always, the family was the foundational model in the corporate community, not vice versa.

Two of the functions of priesthood were immediately manifest in these meetings. First, there was teaching of the Word of God. Second, corporate prayers were offered in the name of all of Israel. Eventually, prayers and acts of piety even came to be viewed as substitutes for the temple sacrifices. This was especially true after the destruction of the temple in 70 A.D., when the rabbis at Yavneh recognized what their fellow Jews–the prophets, Jesus, and the apostles–had come to understand, that worship was not restricted to the temple and was more than sacrifices and offerings.[37]

In the midst of this passion for study and worship, however, a new social order was also emerging. The synagogue became a societal meeting dynamic, a mechanism for social interaction, a true place of meeting. It became a Jewish community center. Biblical human interaction provides for both social relationship, worship, and study. Any worshipping community that neglects any of these three areas is deficient.

Social relationship, study, and worship became the three functions of the synagogue. Eventually, the synagogue became known as a *Beth Knesset* (house of meeting),[38] a *Beth Midrash* (house of study), and a *Beth Tefillah* (house of prayer). In the latter case, the prophetic description of the temple itself[39] became a term of identity for the synagogue. Except for carrying out the sacrificial system, the synagogue had become a mini-temple (*mikdash me'at*) in itself. Indeed, its three functions replicated the distinct areas and furnishings of Israel's wilderness tabernacle as well as the three compartments of Abraham and Sarah's tent. It should

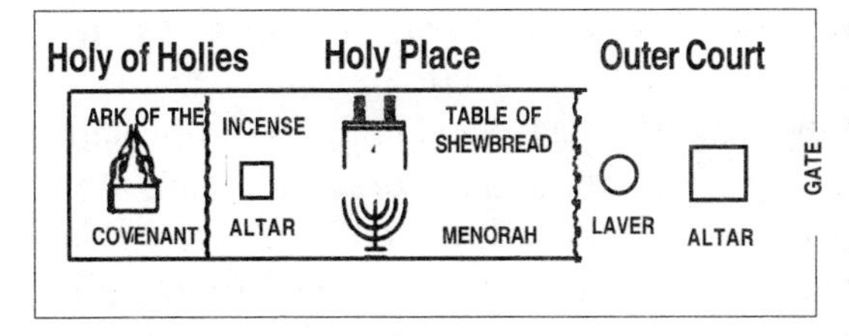

This diagram shows the three distinct divisions of Israel's wilderness sanctuary which replicated the three sections of Abraham's tent home. Every home, like the ancient synagogue should be a house of meeting (Outer Court, the place of meeting), a house of study (the Holy Place with its symbols of the Word of God, the shewbread and the menorah), and a house of prayer (Holy of Holies, the place of worship.)

come as no surprise, then, that the three synagogal functions were the features of earliest Christianity that developed from the matrix of Second Temple Judaism. Jesus and his disciples were not engaged in establishing an alternative priesthood or a new religion for their Jewish family. They simply continued in complete continuity with the religion and the systems in which they had been reared and with which they were totally comfortable. There was no lurching demand for an innovative religious form or substance. They were Jews, their religion was Judaism, and they abandoned neither identity.

What the disciples sought to do was to make their understanding that in the person of Jesus the Messianic expectations of their Jewish family had been fully realized and that God's promise to bring salvation to Israel and the world had brought completion and fulfillment to their ancient system of praise, worship, and service. Large portions of the first-century Jewish community in Israel and abroad came to share this prophetic insight. What eventually came to be thought of as a Gentile religion was in reality one of the most dominant forms of first-century Judaean and Galilean Judaism.

THE SYNAGOGAL MINI-SANCTUARY

The synagogal model was perfectly manifest in the first days of the empowered congregation that eventually came to be known as the church. The disciples' dynamism and impact upon their fellow Jews was said to have been the result of their continuing in the apostles' "teaching," in "fellowship" (including breaking of bread), and in "prayers,"[40] precisely the three functions and appellatives of the synagogue. The earliest Christian believers were steadfast Jews, functioning as a community in a *Beth Midrash* (apostolic teaching), a *Beth Knesset* (fellowship or social interaction), and a *Beth Tefillah* (prayers)–nothing more and nothing less. As they continued in this tradition, "the LORD added to the congregation daily those who were saved," as many as 5,000 in one day! "Myriads" (tens of thousands) of Jewish Pharisees[41] and large numbers of temple priests[42] openly professed their faith in Jesus as Messiah. Additionally, many signs and wonders were done by the apostles in this dynamic community setting.

Another significant development in the earliest church was the fact that the community "broke bread from house to house."[43] The breaking of bread was an ongoing exercise of fellowship within the Jewish community that has been described by theologians as "table fellowship." People gathered around the tables in their homes and shared food and fellowship, study and worship. The Christian synagogue was a house-church movement. Corporate worship was first a family exercise in which other members of the larger community were invited to share food and fellowship in a purely social exercise of community building. Then came the exercises of studying God's Word together and joining in corporate prayers. There was no temple, no cathedral, no church, not even a chapel. There were homes! Family worship was the focus of the earliest congregation of Jesus, the church of Christ.

Leaders emerged from the heads of household, not from a professional clergy class. The earliest trans-local leaders were the apostles themselves who had been trained at the feet of Jesus. They did not, however, see themselves as a replacement for the priesthood in the temple. As a matter of fact, they continued to worship at the temple[44] and even decades after Jesus' ascension recognized the temple priesthood and committed themselves to temple ritual.[45]

Christian Continuity

Neither Jesus nor his apostles intended to create a new religion. They sought only to reform through restoration the religion of their ancestors, the religion that God himself had authored at Sinai and had now perfected at Calvary. They were not attempting to establish a new social or religious order called the church. They *were* continuing in the rich, centuries-old tradition of the Jewish synagogue. More than three decades after Pentecost, the local manifestations of the church were still called synagogues at least among the Jewish Christian diaspora.[46] The word *church*, along with all of its attendant implications, was a Medieval misrepresentation of what the Greek word ἐκκλησία (*ekklesia*) and its Hebrew counterpart קָהָל (*kahal*) meant to Jesus and the apostles. The word *church* that appears in most English version of the Bible should always have been rendered "congregation."

Since the earliest leaders of the church in no way viewed themselves as a new priesthood, they continued as laypersons, servants of the people. The fundamental term applied to all the leaders, including Jesus himself[47] was *diakoneo*, servant or minister.[48] Nowhere in the record of the Apostolic Scriptures are Christian leaders called priests. They functioned in priesthood roles only in the context of synagogal worship, not in the form of temple worship. They fulfilled the priestly functions of teaching and leading in worship; however, they were viewed by others and considered themselves to be servants in the truest synagogal sense.

God's intention from the beginning was that all of Israel would be a "kingdom of priests."[49] Each Israelite was to function as a priest with access to God for himself, then for his family, and finally for the community. When Jesus fulfilled forever the sacrificial and liturgical system of the tabernacle and temple cultus, he became High Priest of a new priesthood of all believers, the "royal priesthood."[50] In order for Jesus to be priest, the order had to revert to its original schema, the one employed by God that had made Melchizedek, the king of Salem, the priest of the Most High God when the Abrahamic faith and religion emerged.[51] God's eternal High Priest was his first and only begotten Son.[52] His priesthood was based in his being the first begotten among many brethren,[53] the head of the family of God. The continuing priesthood of believers was based in its service to the family and the extended family and in roles of leadership in home, synagogue, and congregation.[54]

The principle of the priesthood was manifest in ancient times in the priesthood of the head of the household. It was the responsibility of the head of each family to fulfill the roles of priesthood, to lead the family in matters of social interaction, in matters of study, and in matters of worship and prayer.

THE FAMILY ALTAR

In Jewish homes, the table is more than an appliance for dispensing food. It is an altar. As a matter of fact, the family table is considered to be an altar parallel with that on which the sacrifices were offered in Israel's ancient sanctuaries, both the tabernacle in the wilderness and the temple in Jerusalem. This comparison is established in the fact that the Prophet Malachi described the temple altar as being a *shulchan* (table).[55] If God's altar is his table, the sages reasoned, then man's table must also be an altar. This is why Paul, the rabbi from Tarsus, argued that one could not partake of the Lord's table and the table of demons,[56] comparing the ecclesial altar with the altars in temples that were the focus of idolatrous worship of the Greek pantheon of gods.

Unfortunately in a large portion of modern homes, the table is little more than a feeding trough. Grace is rarely said at the table, and in more and more households, the family almost never gathers as a unit around the table. The table or the bar or even the refrigerator and/or microwave, has become little more than a vending machine in a transportation terminal. Everyone grabs a bite in insolated and silent anonymity and quickly moves on. What few words that are exchanged are yelled over the din of private music piped in through earphones that virtually silence all competition or over the roar of television's mindless, empty laugh tracks. This lack of sanctity for the family table is graphically illustrated in a recent radio commercial for furniture. When the delivery men are told to place the refrigerator in the den next to the television, they wonder, "Won't that make it hard to cook?" The homeowner replies, "Of course not; one of the slots in the home entertainment center is reserved for the microwave!"

Even if the family on occasion eats together, little thought is given to the sacredness of the occasion or of using the time to affirm familial relationships and to strengthen commitment to God. In the modern world, success and pleasure have become the supreme pursuits, the gods to which homage must be paid and endless time devoted. The most valuable of all resources is readily expended upon these empty, unsatisfying deities. What the quest for success does not devour, the lust for pleasure is lurking in the shadows to consume. Nothing is left but the often drug-induced lapse into oblivion that masquerades as sleep.

Understanding the table as an altar elevates mealtime from the mundane to the sublime. The table is not just a food-distribution appliance. It is a sacred place, a spiritual object. What is done there, including the consumption of food, is to be done with reverence and honor to God, the supreme provider. Even eating itself becomes a spiritual exercise, done with the expectation that when one has eaten and is full, he is then to praise the Lord for the bounty of his provision. This was God's first worship instruction to Israel. Israel's first liturgical exercise was to be a prayer of blessing and thanksgiving for God's dietary provision.[57] The God who is blessed at the beginning of the meal as the Sovereign who brings forth bread from the earth is again blessed as the giver of both a good land and the food that it produces.

This most ancient of worship formulae is called in the Jewish community the *Birkath haMazon*. It features a blessing of praise to God for being the one who feeds the entire world. It continues with thanksgiving to God for providing a good and fruitful land with which he constantly sustains his children at every hour. It concludes with a prayer for God to have mercy upon his people Israel and upon Jerusalem and petitions God to continue to feed, nourish, sustain, support, and relieve his people.

A PLACE OF MEETING

The family sanctuary is first a place of meeting. Just as Israel's wildernesss sanctuary was called the tent of meeting, so the family table must become a place of fellowship for the entire family. The home must be a small version of the synagogal *Beth Knesset*, a place for secure interpersonal relationship.

The modern family spends far too little time in interpersonal interaction in the home. Individual time demands upon father, mother, and children are so great that there is no time for corporate familial interaction. Time is gobbled up by life's "important" activities, leaving the family-time plate empty and the relationship cupboard bare. The home has become more a depot than a dwelling. It is like Grand Central Station, where different family members come steaming in on different concourses at different times and then head off in another direction with little more than a nod or a grunt. Then society laments the condition of its youth. Parents are clueless. Even the church seems helpless. Why are children murdering children? Why are young minds fried on drugs? "We don't understand; we've given them everything," parents moan to themselves. The answer is so simple that it is too simple: too many modern parents give everything to their children except time. The average American father currently spends all of two minutes a day with his children!

Each family needs a designated place and specified time for social interaction. Time is needed to talk about the events of life and to listen to one another's needs and concerns. Just like God's children need to meet with him, family members need to meet with one another. Children need quality time on a purely social level with their parents. Other times can be set for instruction and worship exercises. All of life, however, is not wrapped up in these important functions. Time must be made for conversation and interaction so that children can develop the social skills needed for successful life. Meeting around the table in the total absence of entertainment devices and media materials is a vital part of the family sanctuary. When social interaction occurs around a table that is recognized as an altar, it will inevitably be wholesome.

A PLACE OF STUDY

The table as an altar is designed to be a small version of the synagogal *Beth Midrash*, a place for studying God's Word. Herein is manifest another profound Jewish concept that has been largely lost to the Christian understanding: study is worship. Most Christians conceive of worship as something that is done in church with one's eyes closed. Study is recognized as necessary for a successful life; however, it is not generally considered to be worship.

When we analyze the biblical concept of worship, however, we discover that it entails more than enraptured euphoria or existential emotion. The Hebrew word for worship is שָׁכָה (*shachah*), which means to "prostrate oneself" (as in the presence of the Deity). This word graphically demonstrates the ultimate submission that worship demands. The Greek word for worship, προσκυνέω (*proskuneo*), is even more graphic, implying the action of submission parallel with a dog licking its master's hand. True worship is not a struggle to achieve warm fuzzies. It is prostration–lying flat on the ground before God. Every fiber of one's being is submitted to God and his instructions. One may not be required literally to prostrate himself; however, the attitude of the heart must be one of submission to God if true worship is manifest.

Study, therefore, is a high form of worship, for it is study of the Word of God, with a view toward doing the Word, that is the very essence of submission to God. The idea of acquiring knowledge of God's Word with no commitment to doing it is foreign to Judaism. While knowledge of the Word of God for its own sake is the paramount virtue in Judaism, erudition without action is unthinkable. The emphasis is always on the doing. Jews have an insatiable desire to know God's Word, but they also have an unquenchable passion to fulfill it. Greeks study only to know; Jews study in order to know and to revere!

The foundational declaration of Jewish faith, the *Shema* ("Hear, O Israel, the LORD our God, the LORD is one") rests on the word *hear*, a word that means "hear and do."[58] Israel's initial response to God's thundering discourse from Sinai was, "All that you have said, we will do and we will hear [intelligently]."[59] In a supra-logical formula, Israel confessed that they would do and then understand (hear). God's instructions are ineffable. In order to understand them, one must first do them. This, in turn, requires the supreme submission of studying in order to do before understanding comes.

Study in the Jewish home, then, is a high form of worship. It is another of the worship exercises that transpire around the family altar, the table. The bread from the earth is consumed as an exercise that leads immediately into the consumption of the bread from heaven, the living Word of God. Every Christian home would well profit from this example so that mealtime would feature both earthly and heavenly food, nourishing both the outer and the inner man. When this approach is taken, bread from the earth (*lechem min ha-aretz*) becomes bread from heaven (*lechem min ha-shamayim*), the manna of ancient times that was bread from God's table.

One profound, residual benefit of consuming the Word of God is the fact that it strengthens covenantal relationships. The spiritual bonds that cement familial relations are ever strengthened by the ingestion of God's Word. Human relationships are polished to pristine purity by mutual commitment to God's revealed will. Unity that is so much needed in both the domestic scene as well as in the ecclesiastical situation is fostered when individuals come to the full knowledge of God's Son, the person of his Word.[60] Just as the sanctifying truth of God's Word unites disciples of Christ in a unity parallel with that of the Heavenly Father and the divine Son,[61] so the living Word cements the bonds of family solidarity.

Sharing God's Word around the family altar puts everything that is needed on the table to build strong Godly character in all family members. It demonstrates the fact that God's instructions apply to all. Parents are responsible to speak and then to model divine insight before their children so that the children can imitate their parents in lives of faith and purity.

A PLACE OF PRAYER AND WORSHIP

The family table/altar also is designed to be a center for worship, a miniature version of the synagogal *Beth Tefillah*. A relic of pre-modern society is a slogan that still says it all: "The family that prays together stays together." This saying has never been more truly manifest than in the traditional Jewish home, where prayers and blessings are continually spoken, especially around the table. The table is a center for spiritual development as well.

Virtually all of the worship exercises that believers experience in corporate, congregational devotion can be enjoyed in the sanctity of the family sanctuary. Heads of household can lead families as priests in their homes just as leaders of congregations lead their assemblies in worship. Even Christianity's most central recurring sacrament, holy communion, can be shared in the context of family worship, for both its ancient Jewish precursors were family events.

The most prominent antecedent of communion was Passover, which was first celebrated in individual Israelite homes where extended family and friends were invited into the family sanctuary to share the lamb.[62] Jesus himself continued the tradition that he had received from his Jewish family by celebrating the Passover on the night of his betrayal.[63] It was then that he took the unleavened bread and wine of the traditional Passover observance and instituted holy communion by pouring new meaning into the ancient ritual and enjoining his disciples to celebrate Passover thereafter in remembrance of his death.[64] Communion, therefore, was instituted on the night of a Passover that was observed in a family setting.[65]

Communion is also anchored in the weekly *Shabbat* meal, which is introduced by *berachot* (blessings) to God for the provision of wine and bread. The blessings that Jesus himself spoke over the bread and wine were the same benedictions that his ancestors had recited as they celebrated *Shabbat* with their families. As he instituted a new Passover order, Jesus very likely spoke these same time-honored words: "*Barukh attah Adonai, Elohenu, Melekh ha-olam, ha-motzi lechem min ha-aretz . . . Barukh attah Adonai, Elohenu, Melekh ha-olam, borey pri ha-gafen*" (Blessed are you, O Lord our God, King of the universe, who brings forth bread from the earth . . . Blessed are you, O Lord our God, King of the universe, who creates the fruit of the vine." These blessings were given on *Shabbat* first in the context of family and then in corporate worship.

Communion was originally celebrated in the context of family. There was no need for a priest or minister to bless the bread and the fruit of the wine, for neither needed blessing.[66] Both elements of communion are inherently good. They are not profane and do not need to be blessed in order to make them holy. Rather than blessing things, the familial priest is qualified to bless (praise) the Lord, and each participant can discern in the bread and "fruit of the vine" (grape juice or wine) the body and blood of Jesus as he eats and drinks it.[67] The bread and wine of communion can be shared in the family setting at any time that food would normally be consumed in the family sanctuary.

What better way is there to teach children that Jesus is the bread of life and that his blood cleanses from all sin than to "do this in remembrance of [him]" in the intimacy and security of the home? Having so received the communion of the living Christ in their family sanctuary, families are prepared to celebrate and receive the larger community of believers into the continually expanding family circle of the church that is in communion with one another and with the living Lord.

If the most sacred of Christian worship experiences can be shared in the context of the family sanctuary as well as in the corporate sanctuary, virtually any act of worship can be celebrated in the context of the family. What the familial priesthood has administered in the mini-sanctuary is expanded and magnified when the priest-leader of the congregation celebrates in the corporate family sanctuary.

RENEWING THE FAMILY SANCTUARY

Much like Solomon's temple, the family sanctuary has suffered destruction both as a conceptual idea and as a practical reality. Something akin to Babylon has overwhelmed this ancient, biblically Hebraic formula, replacing it almost exclusively with corporate sanctuaries and public worship. Now it is time for a restoration to take place akin to that of the time of Ezra and Nehemiah, of Joshua and Zerubbabel, of Haggai and Zechariah.

The home that has for so long been relegated to a position of relative unimportance as a mere social convention now must be restored to the position of honor that it had in biblical times as a family sanctuary. In a day of growing violence against the fundamental societal unit, it is imperative that both the Jewish and Christian communities hold up the biblical standard in the face of the onslaught. The family must be restored as the center for spiritual and societal development.

Each home must view itself as a sanctuary, a mini-temple in which all the functions of biblical community life have their beginnings and are fully manifest. Doing so will restore a God-consciousness to both the church and society that will transcend the nominal Christian or Jewish experience. It will return the family of God to a face-to-face relationship of walking with God. It will be Eden renewed in the family sanctuary!

Adopting these biblically Hebraic views will empower families to make their homes such powerful sanctuaries of blessing that extended family, friends, and even strangers will welcome the experience of warmth and joy that inclusion in this circle of love affords. By providing familial social interaction, teaching, and worship, the home will become one of the church's most effective agents for evangelism and community development. The church multiply itself by the number of its families, and the kingdom of God will advance through the domestic temple, the family sanctuary.

[1] Genesis 3:8.
[2] Genesis 5:22.
[3] Hebrews 11:5.
[4] Genesis 6:2.
[5] Genesis 6:9.
[6] Genesis 6:8.
[7] Genesis 14:18-19.
[8] Genesis 18:1-10.
[9] Romans 4:11.
[10] Genesis 18:19.
[11] Exodus 12:8, 11, 22, paraphrased.
[12] Exodus 12:3, New International Version.
[13] Exodus 19:6.
[14] Even though the camp of the Israelites moved when the divine cloud that marked the place of the sanctuary moved, the sanctuary was clearly designed to be with the people.

[15] Genesis 35:2.
[16] Exodus 16:15.
[17] 2 Samuel 6:20.
[18] Numbers 6:23.
[19] 2 Samuel 7:5-8.
[20] Psalm 137:2-4.
[21] Israel was commanded to engage in corporate worship exercises in addition to their worship in the context of family. These were the convocations (calling together) which God required of them (cf. Leviticus 23:2). Exercises of family worship never exempt believers from the requirement to assemble together in the corporate sanctuary (Hebrews 10:25). It is in the context of community that worship is fully expressed and accountability is maintained. As a matter of fact, many of the most prominent prayers in the Jewish community cannot be prayed except in the company of ten men, the *minyan* or quorum for prayer. This is also when asked about the size of their congregations, rabbis answer in terms of families, not individuals.
[22] Church as a spiritual entity was first manifest at Sinai. The Greek word that is translated "church" in English versions of the Scriptures is actually ἐκκλησία (*ekklesia*) in the Greek. The word *ekklesia* was used in the Septuagint Greek version of the Hebrew Scriptures (the version most commonly used in the first-century Gentile church) to translate the Hebrew word קָהָל (*kahal*), which simply means "congregation." The *kahal* was the "church in the wilderness" to which Stephen alluded in Acts 7:38.
[23] Hebrews 9:12.
[24] 2 Corinthians 5:20.
[25] Acts 1:8.
[26] Romans 15:16. This passage is accurately rendered, "That I should be the liturgist of Jesus Christ, sacrificing the gospel of God."
[27] Colossians 3:17; 2 Corinthians 4:15.
[28] 1 Peter 2:5; Hebrews 13:16.
[29] 1 Thessalonians 5:17-18.
[30] Hebrews 8:2; 9:24.
[31] 1 Peter 2:5.
[32] 1 Corinthians 6:19.
[33] 1 Timothy 2:5; Hebrews 8:6; 9:15.
[34] 1 Peter 2:9.
[35] Exodus 22:29; Numbers 3:12.
[36] Exodus 20:9.
[37] cf. John 4:21-24; Hosea 6:6; Mark 12:33; Hebrews 10:5-6; 1 Peter 2:5).
[38] An important part of the *Beth Knesset* was the *Beth Din*, the house of judgment. Justice was dispensed in Israel in the context of the community meeting (*knesset*).
[39] Isaiah 56:7.
[40] Acts 2:42.
[41] Acts 21:20.

[42] Acts 6:7.
[43] Acts 2:46.
[44] Acts 3:1; 22:17.
[45] Acts 21:26.
[46] James 2:2. In this passage: "If there come into your assembly a man with a gold ring . . ." the word rendered *assembly* is συναγωγή (*sunagoge*) in Greek and should be translated "synagogue." Since all Christians know that the word *synagogue* can be applied only to the Jews (or to the "synagogue of Satan" as in Revelation 2:9; 3:9), it could never be used as a term to identify a Christian congregation; therefore, translators of the Scriptures have universally rendered the word *sunagoge* in this passage as "meeting," or "assembly."
[47] Romans 15:8.
[48] Ephesians 3:7.
[49] Exodus 19:6.
[50] 1 Peter 2:9.
[51] Hebrews 5:6-10.
[52] Hebrews 1:6; John 1:14.
[53] Romans 8:29.
[54] Though the emphasis in Jewish worship in the synagogue has involved virtually everyone, certain parts of the liturgy have been performed by the *kohanine* ("priests"), those of Aaronide ancestry. These include the pronouncing of the priestly benediction.
[55] Malachi 1:7, 12.
[56] 1 Corinthians 10:21.
[57] Deuteronomy 8:10.
[58] Deuteronomy 6:4.
[59] Exodus 24:7.
[60] Ephesians 4:13.
[61] John 17:17-21.
[62] Exodus 12:4.
[63] Luke 22:15.
[64] Jesus considered his disciples to be his adopted family (cf. Matthew 12:48-50).
[65] 1 Corinthians 11:23-26.
[66] The idea that a priest is required to bless the elements of communion is based in the neo-Platonic and even Gnostic idea that the material is inherently evil and therefore must be "blessed" in order to become "holy" and not profane. The biblical idea is that everything God made was "good" and is to be used for good according to his instructions. The Jewish *berakhot* (blessings) tradition always involves blessing God, not things.
[67] 1 Corinthians 11:29.

Chapter 4

Sanctuaries in Time

KEEPING FAMILY APPOINTMENTS

Sanctuary for a family is very much the same as sanctuary for God. It is created in time, not in space. Just as God never chose to create a physical sanctuary in a geographical location somewhere in the universe and then demand that all worship directed toward him originate from that material structure, so the family should never attach its idea of sanctuary to a specific physical location.[1]

In order to have true family sanctuary, one must be careful to avoid focusing energies on things that appear to promote family well-being but fail to provide enduring havens of secure, affirming relationships. Attractive alternatives to true sanctuary are many and varied, offering the unwary and undiscerning family emphases that are foundations for disillusionment and dissolution of the family. Counterfeits, no matter how attractive or imposing, can never substitute for true family sanctuary.

SHRINES OF MATERIALISM

If one's notion of sanctuary is securely identified with a geographical location or with a physical structure, anything that disturbs that site or shrine or one's attachment to it disrupts, even destroys the sanctuary. Families that make the mistake of attaching their identities to a house or to a certain social connection can find either the structure or the connection suddenly wrenched from them. Such a loss can be devastating, demolishing their corporate domestic identity and shattering their sacred interrelationship.

Parents should be very careful that they themselves understand that success in life and the utopia of security that they seek cannot be assured by material assets, and they should be diligent to teach their children this foundational truth. In an age of glorified materialism, one must be even more diligent to protect against societal imposition of the idea that success is measured by money, power, or prestige.

Such ideas of sanctuary in space have produced the unthinkable. Fathers have murdered their entire families because their image of success was threatened. Mothers have killed their helpless infant children because their personal freedom and social connections were challenged. Children have slaughtered their parents in a blood-lust for instant fortune. Destroying one's most precious relations has been mistakenly viewed as the key to personal success and safety.

At the same time, thousands more have resorted to less murderous means to achieve their own ideas of security, engaging in deception, treachery, and perfidy that have astounded their families and friends. Levels of betrayal have been unthinkable. Children who have been nurtured on false demands for success in families consumed by materialism have sacrificed their familial relationships on the altar of the god *mammon* (unrighteous gain), and the consequences have been devastating to their families and to their own mental health.

INDIVIDUALISM'S INSANE ASYLUM

Modern Western culture has exalted individualism to an almost worshipped state. The result has been a generation intoxicated by the worship of self. Everything is to be sacrificed upon the altar of self-sufficiency, self-generated success. When one politician was reminded by a colleague that a particularly obnoxious, egocentric opponent should be overlooked because he was a "self-made man," his friend remarked, "Thank Goodness, that relieves the Almighty of an awesome responsibility!" Men who pursue their own agendas at the expense of corporate well-being often create history's greatest disasters. Their insane lust for success at any cost destroys both themselves and those around them.

The truth is that though God did create man with free will that permits independent thinking and individual choice, God was not the author of egocentricity and megalomania in man. This is a learned trait, not innate in the human personality as God created it. It stems from the *yetzer ha-ra* (inclination toward evil) that according to rabbinic tradition is inherent in all mankind. The *yetzer ha-ra* involves the instinct for survival and self-preservation, which is good; however, when driven to extreme by Adam's sin and the sin of every subsequent human being, it can lead to selfishness and incredible misanthropy.[2] Individuals who are taught by precept or example that their own rights, wants, and desires supersede the well being of the corporate community of which they are a part will inevitably find themselves imprisoned in an asylum of selfishness.

The ideal of freedom is God's gift to all humanity. It is an inalienable right of every human being. The divine gift, however, can become a curse if taken to the extreme that exalts person and demands that he have power, prestige, and perquisites at the expense of his fellow man. Freedom is both an individual and a corporate right. To remove or diminish either is to destroy the ideal of freedom altogether. To exalt individual right to the level that destroys the rights of the community is to invite autocracy, despotism, anarchy, and/or societal disintegration. To exalt the corporate right so that it destroys individual freedom is to invite the tyranny of a forced uniformity that results in stagnation and death.

The answer to this dilemma is both familial and societal promotion of both individual and corporate identity. This promotion begins in the home, where each child must be challenged to personal achievement. Discerning parents will recognize early on the inclinations and interests of each child, and they will commit their energies to facilitating the child's development toward success in that area. At the same time, however, the parents must underscore the fact that each child is part of a greater whole, first of the nuclear family, then of the extended family, and finally of society in general.

Children must be taught the ethic of ensuring that their efforts toward self-actualization also work toward the betterment of their families and society. The maxim of yesteryear is still applicable today: "God first, others second, and self last." Individual achievements must be weighed in the balances of societal contribution. How do one's accomplishments contribute to the advancement, security, and well-being of humankind?

THE CORPORATE SANCTUARY

The necessity for balancing individual and corporate needs has long been understood by the Jewish community. As a matter of fact, it goes back to the first generations of that family that became the progenitors of the Jewish people, the Israelites. After generations of the assertion of individual rights and the resulting mayhem and murder that accompanied such demands, two siblings were able to subsume their own prerogatives to the benefit of their corporate community. Ephraim and Manasseh were the first brothers who overcame the fratricidal carnage that had brought grief and division to the children of their ancestral families like Cain and Abel and Jacob and Esau, and no doubt hundreds, if not thousands of others.

When their father Joseph brought these siblings to their

grandfather Jacob for the most coveted patriarchal blessing, the head of the Israelite family crossed his hands so that the right hand of blessing rested upon Ephraim rather than upon the firstborn, Manasseh. Despite their father's insistence that he was making a mistake, Jacob continued the benediction that transferred the rights of primogenitor to Ephraim.[3] Manasseh could have reacted violently and sought to protect his birthright; however, both he and his brother learned to subject their own rights to the best interest of the family and community.

As a result of the attitude of deference that was manifest in these brothers, Jacob subsequently commanded that the transgenerational blessing that was to be pronounced by all Israelite fathers upon their sons should begin with these words: "May the Lord make you like Ephraim and Manasseh."[4] Far more illustrious names could be invoked upon the heads of the sons of Israel, including Abraham, Moses, David, and Samuel, but the names that are models for the conduct of Jewish males are Ephraim and Manasseh. The Jewish ideal is the one who has individual rights and aspirations but who also has the wisdom and fortitude to subject those rights and aspirations to what is in the best interest of the family and the community.

A Jew thinks of self only in the context of community. How will one's action affect one's total family? How will it affect his nuclear and extended family? How will it affect his community? How will it affect the entire family of Israel? This mindset is inculcated from infancy in the Jewish consciousness, both individual and corporate. Each child is challenged to achieve, and no level of success is excluded. Whatever the chosen field of endeavor, excellence is the expectation. At the same time, however, the family and community are not sacrificed on the altar of a cult of self-worship. Wealth and power are means for helping advance the well-being of the family and the community.

It should come as no surprise, then, that virtually all of the prayers of the Jewish community are offered in the first person plural. Some sages have even suggested that any prayer that is not offered in the name of the entire Jewish community is no prayer at all. When one enlists the intervention and support of God, it is not merely for self-indulgence or for self-accomplishment and security. It is for the blessing of the community.

Jesus mirrored this Jewish mindset when he instructed his disciples to pray: "*Our* Father . . . give *us* . . . forgive *us* . . . lead *us*. . ."[5] These immortal words of the "Lord's Prayer" are merely a synopsis of ancient synagogal prayer formulae that predated the time of Jesus and were, indeed, the focus of his own personal and corporate prayer life. Jesus even took the ideal of corporate responsibility to a level higher than that of his contemporaries in first-century Jewish society, suggesting that the highest ideal was that one should lay down his own life for his family and community.[6] Then, he personally demonstrated the truth that he taught by sacrificing himself for the redemption of the human family from the bondage of sin and death.[7]

Jesus subjected his will that he escape suffering to the Father's will that all men should come to repentance and receive the gift of eternal life.[8] He could have asserted his right to life because, unlike all men who had lived before him, he did not deserve to die because he had never sinned and was, therefore, not subject to sin's penalty.[9] He could rightly have demanded the sanctuary of his own safety, summoning legions of angels to deliver him from pain and suffering.[10] Instead, like Manasseh of old, he recognized what was in the best interest of his family, the family of man, and freely sacrificed all his rights.[11] As a result, God has exalted him and given him a name above every name.[12]

God's idea of sanctuary, then, is not in rugged individualism and personal accomplishment. One discovers the safest place in the world when he aligns himself with God's will to pursue the benefit and blessing of family and community. Christians are commanded to love one another with the same degree of self-sacrificial devotion with which Jesus loved humanity.[13] True security is found in mutually submitted relationships void of self-aggrandizement.[14] True sanctuary is in familial community.

TIME, THE ULTIMATE SANCTUARY

In reality, the only true sanctuary is one that is built in time.[15] This is the one sanctuary that God himself built: a time capsule. He did so at the conclusion of his act of creation. The last thing that God made was a sanctuary, a temple in time. After six days of creative activity, God set apart for all eternity the seventh day as time for relationships. He created a sanctuary in time, the Sabbath.

Time is the one thing that cannot be destroyed by enemies. It is the one thing that cannot be eroded by elements or obliterated by nature's convulsive and cataclysmic upheavals. No matter what the physical situation, one can withdraw into the sanctuary of time to worship the Creator and to be with family and community. Each person controls what he does with time.

Tyrants can destroy temples, civic centers, and homes; however, they cannot destroy time. Though imprisoned and tormented, men can set apart a temporal sanctuary. This sanctuary costs nothing in terms of material resources. It costs everything, however, in terms of personal commitment to divine instruction. This sanctuary in time demands ongoing, week-by-week renewal of determination to give God and family the time that he, they, and oneself require.

This is why God sanctified and blessed the Sabbath. As a matter of fact, the Sabbath is the only immaterial thing that he ever blessed.[16] God recognized that the creation would need a sanctuary for repose, a medium for renewal and worship. It is for this reason that one-seventh of the divine energy of creation was expended on generating rest.[17] Perhaps this is because one of the most difficult things for men to do is to rest and enjoy God and family. At any rate, God considered this exercise so important that he devoted one-tenth of his thundering words of divine instruction to the command: "Remember!"[18]

The sages of Israel observed that the text of Holy Scripture declares God finished his work "on the seventh day."[19] Since everything material was either created out of nothing or was formed during the first six days of creation, what, they wondered, was the work that God finished on the seventh day? The only conceivable answer was that on the seventh day, God created *menuchah* (rest, repose). *Menuchah* in Hebrew comes from *nuach*, which means "to stop." Likewise, *Shabbat* (Sabbath) is from the root *shevet* which literally means "to sit down." The fundamental concept of *Shabbat* then is that of cessation.

The idea behind the Sabbath is not entirely physical rest, even though it is a significant part of fulfilling the divine commandment to remember God's set-apart day. The underlying idea is that of cessation. God simply designed the creation in such a way that every seven days, everything should stop, and time should be set apart for God and family.

There is ever a need for a divine whole rest to be imposed on the staff of life amidst the swelling crescendos of feverish notes struggling above the scale for success or amongst ominous tones plummeting below the staff into the depths of failure, defeat, and depression. Someone has suggested tongue-in-cheek that when Jesus invited his disciples to "come apart and rest,"[20] he meant that if they did not rest they would come apart. The exegesis may not be sound, but the idea is! Human restlessness can be satisfied only by divine rest.

MAKING APPOINTMENTS

More important than rest, however, is the Sabbath's sanctuary of time that provides and promotes relationship with God and with family, both the immediate nuclear family and the corporate human family. Once each week, every family needs a retreat from the pressures of everyday life. Special time has to be set apart. The human tendency is to rush onward and upward, struggling to go where no man has gone before. Unbridled ambition does not automatically provide for cessation. Only when one fully recognizes the importance of temporal sanctuary will provision be made for its establishment and maintenance.

In the Jewish *Shabbat*, time is made for everyone. First, a divine appointment is kept. Sabbath is the first of God's *mo'edim* (appointments).[21] God himself has set apart this time on his calendar to meet with his family. When God's children match this divine appointment with time set apart on their calendars, a miracle of spiritual renewal and physical regeneration takes place.

This is why God made time management one of his ten preeminent instructions for the human race. "Remember the Sabbath to keep it set apart,"[22] he commanded. God realized from the moment of man's creation that time management was as important to human well-being as was avoiding murder, theft, and adultery. The truth that man usually does not understand is that more can be accomplished in six blessed days than in seven unblessed. When one-seventh of time is set apart for God and family, one is renewed, and the works of his hand are blessed. The same is true for money, the counterpart of time. More can be accomplished with 90 percent blessed than with 100 percent unblessed. With time, one-seventh is God's; with money, one-tenth is his.

Rest for rest's sake, however, is not the fullness of the Sabbath. The building and nurturing of relationship is its essence. First, one builds, renews, and strengthens relationships with the Creator, understanding and confirming that existence and sustenance are not self-generated but are the result of divine providence. God is man's source; therefore, the believer has no hesitation in following God's instruction that to cease from labors for livelihood and rest in God's provision. Setting apart one day out of seven specifically for worship in a holy convocation to a divine appointment confirms and strengthens man's vertical relationship with God.

At the same time, however, Sabbath is no more restricted to worship directed toward God than it is restricted to total cessation from any physical activity. Sabbath is also time for family. Many Christians have missed this important truth and have preoccupied themselves with the work of rest and worship on their Sabbath and have found themselves exhausted at its end. They have worked so hard at *keeping* the Sabbath that they have failed to *delight* in this sanctuary in time. Jesus well observed that it is lawful to do good on the Sabbath day.[23]

The Jewish people, being the longest and most faithful celebrators of God's Sabbath, have discovered the enriching experience of the true sanctuary in time. The focus of the Jewish *Shabbat* is on the family, first the nuclear family and then the extended corporate family. For Jewish families, the Sabbath begins in the home. Father, mother, and children retreat from the hustle and bustle of everyday life into the sanctuary of the Sabbath and even invite guests to join them in the family sanctuary that has assembled in time.

As the sun sets on Friday evening, the Jewish family leaves the challenges of ordinary life and enters its sanctuary, the Sabbath. The door to the frenetic activity of life closes, shutting out the ordinary, closing in the divine. As the mother lights candles welcoming both the Sabbath and the divine presence into the home, the family sanctuary of safety, security, and peace is reconstituted so that in the Jewish home each family member basks in the warm glow of affirmation and blessing.

Why does such solidarity exist in Jewish families and in the Jewish community in general? The answer is that family bonding takes place on a regularly scheduled basis. Sabbath offers a weekly opportunity to renew and strengthen relationships and to underscore relationship with the living God in the context of the family and community. Synagogue experience is not a performance-based exercise that preserves anonymity. It, too, reaffirms relationships of each family in the larger community.

The Jewish family and the Jewish community are blessed because they spend one-seventh of their time in their temporal sanctuary, cloistered from the pressures of the world about them, basking in loving, supportive relationships and thinking of their blessedness as God's chosen people. Because they have been engaging one another and God in the intimacy of their homes, congregational gatherings are celebrations of life and the opportunity to worship God together as an extended family and community.

God's Appointments with His Family

Because humans are inherently forgetful and because they become so caught up in the routine of life that demands more and more of their time, God has devised a system of remembrance. The divine principle that requires remembrance is codified in one of the ten words of instruction from Sinai that are commonly called the Ten Commandments. "Remember!" the fourth of these instructions demands. This divine imperative is one of ten categories of commandments that are essential for walking with God by following his instructions for successful living.

The specific remembrance that is commanded in this instruction is to set apart the Sabbath as a memorial of creation (the general command for all humanity) and as a memorial of deliverance from Egyptian bondage (the specific command for the Jewish people).[24] Setting apart one day in seven as a time devoted entirely to God and to family is vital to human health and to human spiritual welfare; however, it is only part of God's remembrance plan.

God's calendar includes daily, weekly, monthly, seasonal, and generational appointments that he has made for meetings with his children. Scripture has always understood that time must be planned, scheduled, and set apart for family; therefore, it has made provision for a systematic outline for "time out" from life's routine that provides opportunity for the most important things in human existence: relationships. Interpersonal relationship is both vertical and horizontal, for God's design is that time be spent in communion first with him, then with family and community. The only way to ensure that this will occur is to establish set times.[25]

First, God has established daily hours of prayer. These set times for God to meet with his children are morning, noon, and evening. In antiquity, they were 9 a.m., noon, and 3 p.m. The morning and afternoon hours of prayer coincided with the required times of sacrifice in the tabernacle and temple. King David observed the three hours of prayer, saying that he was faithful to pray "morning, at noon, and evening."[26] Centuries later, these were the same three times a day when the prophet Daniel prayed in Babylon with his window open toward Jerusalem.[27] His absolute and unequivocal determination to meet God's daily prayer appointments landed him in the king's den of lions.

The tradition of praying three times a day continued among the Jewish people and was a prominent feature in the life of Jesus and the apostles. As a matter of fact, the only place in the Bible where the term *hour of prayer* is specifically mentioned is Acts 3:1 that describes the daily life of the apostles. A cursory review of apostolic events, however, reveals a continuing compliance with the outline for daily prayer that David and Daniel practiced. Jesus was crucified at 9 a.m., the morning hour of prayer,[28] darkness covered Jerusalem at the noon hour of prayer,[29] and Jesus expired at 3 p.m., the afternoon hour of prayer.[30] The Holy Spirit was given to the church on the day of Pentecost at the morning hour of prayer.[31] Peter was praying at the noon hour of prayer when he received the commission to take the gospel to the household of Cornelius,[32] who had been visited by the angel at the morning hour of prayer.[33] Paul received his divine visitation on the Damascus road at the noon hour of prayer.[34]

Throughout their history, the Jewish people have continued to honor the hours of prayer. To this day, they remain faithful to the ancient biblical formula, praying three times a day: *Shacharit* (in the morning), *Mincha* (in the afternoon), and *Ma'ariv* (in the evening). The daily prayer appointments that God has established on his calendar for meeting with his children have been much valued throughout salvation history, and they continue to be important in the Jewish community. Christians, too, can share in this prophetic and apostolic practice, thereby fulfilling Paul's instructions that they "pray without ceasing."[35] Believers who propose to walk daily in the presence of God will readily apply the divine principle of remembrance that establishes three set times for prayer daily.

God's weekly divine appointment is *Shabbat*. Many have suggested that Paul's instructions in Romans 14:5 suspended the responsibility for Sabbath remembrance from all believers, particularly Gentiles. While it is true that no one's salvation or relationship with God can be judged by the days he observes or does not observe or by the manner in which he observes them,[36] it is also true that God's instruction regarding *Shabbat* has never been abrogated. We have Jesus' personal word on it! "Think not that I have come to destroy the law or the prophets. I have not come to destroy but to fulfill,"[37] he declared. Making every day exactly the same (as some have interpreted the Romans text) results in a kind of pansabbathism, which in effect is to have no Sabbath at all. If every day is the Sabbath, then no day is the Sabbath. Instead of spending endless amounts of energy trying to explain away God's instructions, believers would be better served by simply adopting Israel's reaction to the divine wisdom: "Whatever you have said, we will do,"[38] and begin to set apart one day in seven for God and family.

Israel also has a monthly appointment with God called *rosh chodesh*, the new moon. This is another time to stop and consider that God is the author of everything including time. For believers the first of each month would be a good opportunity to evaluate their walk with God during the previous month and to make plans and commitments for the next month. If monthly reevaluation is good for business, how much more is it healthy for the family. This is far better than New Year's resolutions that can be forgotten within weeks only to be dusted off and weakly reaffirmed a year later.

God's chosen people were also given three major seasonal appointments that were expanded into seven and finally into nine. God's three festivals are Passover, Pentecost, and Tabernacles.[39] Ancillary to these are Unleavened Bread and Firstfruits (around the time of Passover) and Trumpets and the Day of Atonement (near the time of Tabernacles). Later, the Jewish people added Purim to celebrate their victory over a genocidal attempt against them in the days of Queen Esther. Then, they began to observe Hanukkah to memorialize their victory over a vicious attempt to destroy Judaism through assimilation into Hellenism during the time of the Maccabees. The biblical festivals are specifically called *mo'edim* (appointments) in the Hebrew Scriptures[40] and are scheduled meetings between God and his children.

Finally, God made generational appointments with his people, including the Sabbath year when all things return to their natural state every seventh year.[41] Additionally, there is a year of jubilee that occurs every 50 years (seven Sabbath years plus one).[42] This is a year of release when all debts are paid and everyone in society is returned to a state of equality.

God's calendar, then, provides for a series of appointments that impact all of human life. The wise will consider

God's instruction to "remember" by employing the divine calendar to meet with God, with family, and with community. Rather than devise one's own calendar, practicality would suggest that it would be more efficient simply to adopt and utilize God's appointment calendar.

FAMILY APPOINTMENTS

If God thought it was important to establish set times of remembrance to meet with his children, how much more should Christian parents understand the need to make appointments with one another, with their children, and with their extended family and community. Making time is essential to health and happiness. Those who fail to make appointments end up lamenting with the popular song, "Gee, ain't it funny how time slips away." Those who follow God's leadership by making daily, weekly, seasonal, and generational appointments to meet with God, with family, and with community find that spiritual growth and healthy interpersonal relationships result.

Just as God has made appointments on his calendar, however, man must also establish set times for himself and his family. Time must be made for God and family. Otherwise, it will be consumed by time-depleting, self-absorbed human nature. One wakes up too late to wonder, "Where did all the time go?" The Romans recognized the fleeting nature of time in their oft-repeated maxim, "*Tempus fugit*" ("time flies"). Unless one makes a conscious and concerted effort to set time apart, it will all become a blur, with one moment indistinguishable from the other and in the end, all seemingly wasted.

First, every family should establish set times daily for family interaction. The specific hour is not nearly as important as the fact that a time or times are set. Schedules vary from family to family; therefore, what is most convenient should be adopted. Exacted, punctilious observance is not as vital as fulfilling divine principles. The important thing is to establish specific daily times for family, preferably morning, noon, and evening. The exercise need not be laborious and extended. A simple, short Bible reading, a prayer, and/or a social exchange between spouses and between parents and children, if done on a consistent basis, will become a much anticipated event. This can easily be done in the morning before work and school, at noon before lunch, and in the evening before bed-time. If set times are established each day, fathers will make more time for communicating with their children. Growth will occur, and family solidarity and unity will ensue.

In addition to daily family appointments, parents must establish set times for their own personal interaction. Children must be made to understand that father and mother are also husband and wife and that their relationship must also be nurtured with set times. A locked bedroom door establishes the fact that there is an intimacy between father and mother that is different from other family relationships. It establishes an inner sanctum in the family sanctuary and confirms to spouses that their intimacy is so valued as to be nurtured in the time sanctuary of appointments made specifically for one another.

Second, weekly time(s) must be set apart for family and God. *Shabbat* is a good time for this interaction, a time for family fellowship, study, worship, and blessing. If Friday evening is inconvenient for the family, another time can be substituted; however, working toward making time that corresponds with God's calendar is a good idea. During this weekly family day, heads of household should assume God-given roles of priesthood to lead families in things pertaining to one another and to God.

Third, it would be very helpful for each family to meet together around the first of each month to review their progress, to see how they have done in maintaining family unity and keeping their family sanctuary secure and strong. Each family can choose when and how to do this. Time and method of observance can be very fluid, designed to meet the need of each individual family. What is important is that everyone stops periodically to remember, to reevaluate, and to renew.

Forth, seasonal appointments can be made that underscore family solidarity by remembering salvation history, studying God's Word, and worshipping together as a family unit. God's festivals have family significance and application and can be observed first in family and then in the context of community. These can be much-anticipated yearly exercises that bring family and friends together for special times of celebration that are more than the usual weekly events.

Generational appointments can be wide and varied. Besides a year of jubilee celebration, various rites of passage in family life can be generational appointments to share quality time with one another and with God. These can include confirmations or *bar/bat mitzvahs* at the time when children reach puberty. They can be graduations, weddings, wedding anniversaries, family reunions, and other important family events. Again, the important thing is not the specific event but that appointments are made and kept.

Time Management

Establishing and maintaining family appointments takes work. If no one is diligent to insist that the appointments are kept, they will degenerate to the point that they will be nonfunctional and meaningless. The second law of thermodynamics, called the law of entropy, establishes the scientific fact that anything left to itself without the constant intervention of an outside force will become less ordered and will degenerate into a state of inert uniformity. Somebody has to do something to set the action in motion, and someone has to do something to maintain its operation. There is no such phenomenon as perpetual motion. For every effect, there must be a cause. Spouses must, therefore, act to establish and maintain set times before their union is blessed with children. Then, they must keep their appointments and see that their children remember them as well.

Time is not an enemy if one sets apart what God has requested. Appointments are established as a divine principle. Those who propose to engage in *imitatio Dei* or who seek to be truly *Christian* will follow the Father's example in setting and maintaining appointments for God and family. In so doing, the family sanctuary will be a temple in time where materialism matters little and relationship is everything!

In an era when virtually everyone has a business calendar and most have laptop or hand-held computers to manage time and remind them of important business appointments, how much more should Christians have a predetermined calendar that reminds them of the most important things that they have in their lives, the times that they spend with God and their families.

To do otherwise is to invite chaos, for one who does not plan and manage time will be consumed by the demands of time that will simply overwhelm him and make it virtually impossible to have spontaneous, quality family time. He will only react to the disasters and problems of life that will inevitably come. Average people wait and react; successful people plan and act. If believers will plan and manage their time like God does, they will discover that it is not as difficult as they thought to build a temple in time, a dimension of fellowship, study, and worship that strengthens the bonds of relationship both with God, with family, and with community in the family sanctuary.

[1] The material sanctuary that God commanded was the tabernacle, a portable structure that accompanied the people. The temple that became the focus of Judaism during the monarchy and afterward was the result of King David's passion to build a sanctuary for God. Jesus declared that the ideal for worship was not in any mountain, including the temple mount, but in spiritual truth manifest in human hearts (cf. John 4:21-23).

[2] Rabbinic thought suggests that there are two inclinations in each human

being, an inclination toward good (*yetzer tov*) and an inclination toward evil (*yetzer ha-ra*). Even the evil inclination has a good element in that it involves survival instincts; however, if not controlled by the inclination toward good, even these elements necessary for human existence can become perverted and used by Satan to foment incredible evil in the world. The conflict between the two *yetzers* in every human heart is the battle in the mind described by Paul in Romans 7:16-20 and 2 Corinthians 10:5. It is the spiritual warfare in which every believer engages.

[3] Genesis 48:14.

[4] Genesis 48:20.

[5] Matthew 6:9-13.

[6] John 15:13.

[7] Hebrews 2:14-15.

[8] Luke 22:42.

[9] Romans 6:23; 2 Corinthians 5:21.

[10] Matthew 26:52-54.

[11] Genesis 48:14; Philippians 2:6-8.

[12] Philippians 2:9-10.

[13] John 13:34.

[14] Ephesians 5:21.

[15] The idea of a sanctuary in time rather than in space is founded on the principle established by Rabbi Abraham Joshua Heschel and powerfully presented in his superb book, *The Sabbath* (New York: Farrar, Strauss, and Giroux). While the principle is anchored in the Sabbath, it also extends to other set times for family and God which we have discussed here.

[16] Exodus 20:11.

[17] Genesis 2:2.

[18] Exodus 20:8.

[19] Genesis 2:2.

[20] Mark 6:31.

[21] Leviticus 23:2-3.

[22] Exodus 20:8.

[23] Mark Matthew 12:9-12; Mark 3:1-3.

[24] Two delineations of the Ten Commandments are given in Scripture. The first enjoins Sabbath observance because God created the universe in six days and rested on the seventh (cf. Exodus 20:8-11). This version, the command to remember weekly that God–not nature or some other force or happenstance–is the creator of everything that exists, is incumbent upon all humanity. The second requires Sabbath observance of the Israelites because they were slaves in Egypt and were delivered by the hand of God (Deuteronomy 5:12-15).

[25] One of the Hebrew words translated "feasts" or "festivals" is *mo'edim*, which means "set times" or "appointments."

[26] Psalm 55:17.

[27] Daniel 6:10-13.

[28] Mark 15:25.
[29] Mark 15:33.
[30] Matthew 27:46.
[31] Acts 2:15.
[32] Acts 10:9.
[33] Acts 10:3.
[34] Acts 22:6.
[35] 1 Thessalonians 5:17.
[36] Colossians 2:16.
[37] Matthew 5:17.
[38] Exodus 24:7.
[39] Exodus 23:14-17; Deuteronomy 16:16; .
[40] Leviticus 23:2.
[41] Exodus 23:11.
[42] Leviticus 25:10.

Chapter 5

A Hut or a Palace

What Is Really Important?

Very often in Western culture, home is associated with the physical structure in which a family dwells. Families are judged and even judge themselves by the quality of their domicile. Those who live in mansions or palaces are thought to be the most successful families. They are imagined to have the "good life." Indeed, the focus of families can become increasingly competitive, the "keeping-up-with-the-Jones" syndrome. Instead of being utilitarian, houses have become badges of success.

The First Home Was a Garden!

Modern society, like many ancient peoples, worships the gods of materialism and pleasure. "He who dies with the most toys wins," trumpets one bumper sticker. Individuals and families are judged more by the quantity of their possessions than by the quality of their character. The good life is measured by hedonism's standards for *joie de vivre*. Madison Avenue magnates and mavens blast everyone continually with the secret to success, which everyone knows is simply purchasing and possessing the one indispensable thing or enjoying the one pleasure that they are advertising.

The result of this subtle ploy of materialism is that extraordinary time, energy, and resources that could have been expended upon family relationships are wasted on material things that more often than not rapidly become expendable. Yesterday's must-have treasure is today's yard-sale junk. "The only difference between men and boys is the price of their toys," and "A woman's place is in the mall," are popular sayings today. The distraction is so subtle that it is often unrecognizable. What makes men and women feel good about themselves is usually an external status symbol or something that brings momentary pleasure.

How is a Christian family to escape being consumed in this Venus fly-trap of commercialism and hedonism? How can one get off the treadmill of endless and mindless efforts to match one's neighbor with the accoutrements of success? How can a family focus on the home and not on the house? There is an answer, and, as usual, it is in the Bible!

God has long had a powerful solution to this dilemma in his system of praise, worship, and service that came to be called Judaism. It dates back over 35 centuries to the time when he established a constitution for his family, the Israelites. After God had liberated the family of Jacob from Egyptian bondage, he established a liturgical order for annual holy days and festivals that would help his people remember his deliverance and their proper or appropriate relationship with him. These were to be divine appointments on God's calendar for times that he would meet with his people and they would meet with one another.

God's appointment calendar began with Passover,[1] proceeded through Pentecost,[2] and concluded with Ingathering (later called Tabernacles).[3] Since Israel was predominantly an agrarian society, God ordained festivals at both the beginning and the end of the harvest season to remind his people that their existence as a social and political entity was wholly dependent upon God's sovereign act of deliverance and upon his continuing provision for their sustenance.

God's system was designed to help the Israelites escape the siren song of self-sufficiency that would attempt to draw them away from dependence upon and devotion to God. If they maintained his celebration system, they would have constant reminders that their identity was not in the things they possessed nor in the power they wielded but in their relationship with God. Each Israelite was to celebrate the Passover by declaring that he himself was a slave in Egypt and that he, not just his ancestors, was personally delivered by God's hand. He was to see himself as standing at Sinai on Pentecost and receiving God's Torah of instructions and guidelines for life. He himself was the recipient of God's bounty in the midst of the most abject of circumstances possible. He was to understand that he himself had lived in flimsy tents on the way to the land of milk and honey.

The Sukkah Experience

During the celebration of the Festival of Ingathering at the end of the year, the Jewish people were commanded to construct huts outside their houses and to dwell in these minimal temporary shelters for an entire week. The hut that each family was to build was called in Hebrew a *sukkah.* From this term came the most prominent name of the autumnal festival, *Sukkot* (Tabernacles or Booths).

Now, this was just the opposite of what human reason would have established for a fall festival. One would have thought that God would have had them surround themselves with the symbols of bounty, dress in finery, gather in ornate temples, and really celebrate the "good life," flitting from party to party, reveling in wine, gourmet food, and sexual dalliance -precisely the experiences prescribed for the autumnal fertility rites of the pagan deities. What better way to celebrate a beneficent God than to revel in the symbols of his bounty! Even today one might think that such a celebration would require giving honor to excess and paying homage to pleasure.

For Israel, however, it was just the opposite: "Build a bare minimalist structure and live in it for a week," God said. Irrational? No, supra-rational! The focus of God's people was not to be on things. It was to be on family and God. Things did not sustain their existence. God did! Their most important possessions were not their houses, lands, or material resources. It was God and the families he had given them. They were not fixated on things. They were focused on relationships!

The celebration of the concluding festival of the liturgical year has been for the Jews a constant reminder of the transient nature of human existence. James observed that life is like a vapor that vanishes into thin air.[4] Solomon lamented that everything under the sun is vanity.[5] When one is periodically reminded of life's evanescence, it is easier to maintain focus on priorities. God in his wisdom has provided a yearly reminder of these truths for those who are observant of his system of worship. Human tragedies underscore what is really important, but God's people do not wait for tragedy. They are reminded yearly, monthly, weekly, and daily!

The *sukkah* also reminded Israel of the transitoriness of structures which can be obliterated in a moment's time in cataclysmic natural disasters like storm, flood, fire, or earthquake. They can also be lost virtually overnight because of economic upheavals. Only one thing in life is more certain than the proverbial "death and taxes" and that is God and his all-sufficient provision for his children. The minimalist hut called the *sukkah* reinforces in the modern mind that structures that seem secure can literally evaporate into thin air.

What is really important in life? What are the things that one can take with him beyond the grave? The material objects deemed so important that family relationships and moral and ethical standards are sacrificed in order to gain them end up in estate sales and are fodder for family arguments and divisions after one passes away. On the other hand, family relationships are the treasures that endure even beyond the grave. Children and grandchildren are a ticket to the future. It is only through them that the living are able to propel their values and memories into the future.[6]

When one eats, sleeps, and engages in family life in a hut for a week each year, opportunity is created to sort out priorities and maintain focus. The hut experience is good for humankind. It reflects the truth of where humans could be if it were not for God's bountiful provision.

Amazingly, Israel's *sukkah* experience has never been considered a burden. It has been seen as a part of the greatest festival of all and has been called the "Season of our Joy," the most wonderful festival of the year. It is also seen as a universal celebration that bids all mankind, both Jew and Gentile, to come together and rejoice in the bounty of God's blessings.

The festival seasons of Scripture are special times for opening the family sanctuary to the strangers, orphans, widows, and the poor. This exercise protected the Jewish family sanctuary from becoming introverted, elitist, and exclusive. God specifically commanded it: "You shall rejoice in your festival, with your son and daughter . . . the stranger, the fatherless and the widow in your communities."[7] The great Talmudist Moses Maimonides expanded this concept: "One who locks the doors to his courtyard and eats and drinks with his wife and children, without giving anything . . . to the poor and bitter in soul–his meal is not 'the joy of the commandment,' but the joy of his stomach. . . . Rejoicing of this kind is a disgrace."[8]

A Christian Tabernacles

Jesus himself celebrated this integral part of his biblical heritage. It was on the last great day of the Festival of Tabernacles that he stood up in the temple complex and proclaimed, "If anyone is thirsty, let him come to me and drink."[9] His offer no doubt coincided with the water libation that was a central part of the Tabernacles experience for the corporate Jewish community. This festival echoed with cries of *Hoshanah*! (God save us), an exclamation of praise to the coming King.

Though it had important corporate significance, the Tabernacles experience was, like virtually every other worship exercise in Judaism, a family affair. In ancient Israel, there was profound, ecstatic worship in the Temple and a liturgical order for the community's interaction. Blazing menorahs, spectacular dancing, and solemn ritual brought excitement to Jerusalem. But, the focus was on the family hut, with each family celebrating its dependence upon God. Even today, among the Jews the focus remains on the family.

The *sukkah* experience can also be shared in the Christian community. Corporate worship exercises can be carried out to encourage rejoicing in God's bounty and his provision for his children. This is a good time to celebrate both salvation history and eschatological expectation. Corporate worship can be as eventful and celebratory as it was in ancient Israel.

The focus, however, should be on the family and those welcomed into its sanctuary, not just on a public corporate demonstration. Christian families can also profit from God's instructions to their ancient Israelite forbears. They can build huts outside their houses, gather in them as family units, and remember that life on earth is only temporary and that eternal bliss in the presence of God awaits those who are faithful to his will. Spending a few nights in a hut will underscore the bounty that the family enjoys and will help each member to understand that what is important in his life is not possessions but relationships, both with God, with family, and with community.

For a family that is wholly dependent upon the clergy for its worship experience, such an exercise may seem impossible. "Why can't the pastor build a hut as a model so we can see it and get the idea and go home?" they might moan. Those accustomed to performance-based religion might think this is the only way they can profit from the Tabernacles lesson.

Those who have restored the family sanctuary to their personal experience, however, will find the Tabernacles experience a natural expression of their already- existing family worship agenda. If God said it, it must be profitable. Indeed, the Word works! Just do it! When the Tabernacles season comes in the autumn of the year, build a hut outside your home. What the neighbors think doesn't matter. In fact, if you do it right, you may just get an opportunity to witness to your faith and share the value of this annual biblical opportunity to reaffirm your priorities.

What you have been doing in your home throughout the year, in engaging in family time for social interconnectivity, you can do in your hut. What you have done in studying God's Word together can be a fresh, invigorating experience in your hut. What you have been doing in praying and worshipping together can be powerfully strengthened as you peer through the branches of the flimsy shelter, view the stars, and with Israel of old envision the coming of the Messiah. You can even pretend with your children that you are on the wilderness journey, bound for the Promised Land.

Just as the father or head of household in ancient Israel killed the lamb and led his family in the Passover celebration, you can lead your family in the yearly Passover by honoring the Paschal Lamb slain from the foundation of the world who redeemed mankind from sin and death. Likewise, you can lead your family in celebrating God's provision of his Word at Sinai and his Spirit at Zion as you memorialize Pentecost, imagining that you, too, heard God's thundering voice proclaim his commandments and that you likewise can experience anew the infilling of the Holy Spirit. Finally, you can lead your family in celebrating the festival of festivals, the feast of joy, ingathering, Tabernacles. And you can do it in your family sanctuary, moved from the security of your home to the flimsy hut that God requested.

CONSTRUCTING YOUR OWN FAMILY SUKKAH[10]

Among the Jewish people, it is considered a *mitzvah* (a good deed in fulfillment of a divine commandment) to build one's own *sukkah* (hut). While it is a part of God's instruction to Israel, it is also a good object lesson for Christian families.

The Feast of Tabernacles comes in the fall of the year (usually in late September or early October). If you want to have your celebration coincide with that of the Jewish people, consult a Jewish calendar for the exact time.

Start your plans a few weeks before the time to build comes. You will need to devise a plan for size and materials. The *sukkah* can be any size as long as it is large enough to sit inside. A good size is around seven feet in length, width, and height.

Since the *sukkah* is meant to be a temporary hut, you can use materials that are lightweight and easy to handle. It is best to use four posts (2 x 2's are fine) for the corners. Four additional poles can be used for the roof. All of these poles need to be around eight feet in length.

In order to cover the roof, you will need small boards capable of supporting light tree branches. For the sides, cloth hangings are preferred though other materials including canvas, cane matting, cardboard, or thin plywood will do. Three sides should be enclosed, and the fourth side should be covered with a cloth drape in order to have an entrance. (An existing building wall may serve as one side of your *sukkah*.) Then, on top you can place a few small tree branches.

Corner posts can be anchored as uprights in the holes of concrete blocks or with stacked bricks or other material. The four 2 x 2's that form the roof square can be nailed together and then attached to the tops of the posts. Once the frame is constructed, place cloth or other materials to cover three sides. Attach a bed sheet or similar material on a wire track at the top of the side you want to use as a door. Finally, place palm or other tree branches on top, being careful to leave openings so that while sitting in the *sukkah* at night you can still see the stars.

You can furnish your *sukkah* to your own taste, with table and chairs or other items. You can add decorations of pictures or other items. Fruit can be hung from the ceiling to emphasize the festive Tabernacles season.

You should certainly involve your children in the construction and decoration of your *sukkah*. This is an excellent time for them to learn the process and share in the excitement with their own creativity.

After you have constructed your *sukkah*, you can assemble family and friends in this "tabernacle" for fellowship, study, prayer, and worship. Try having a meal together in the *sukkah*. You might even want to spend a night there. If the weather is inclement, be safe and healthy and spend the time in your home; however, if the weather is good, spend some time in this temporary enclosure searching the heavens and expressing your expectation of the coming of the Messiah.

Above all, remember that God has committed himself to meeting with his children at the time of this divine appointment. Remember also that life is a vapor that soon passes away and renew afresh your understanding of the things in life that are truly important: your personal relationship with God, your personal relationship to your family, your personal relationship within the body of Christ, the community of believers, and your personal relationship with friends and neighbors in the entire human family, and you can celebrate all of your blessings in the setting of your family sanctuary.

[1] Exodus 12:11-48.
[2] Exodus 19:1-23.
[3] Exodus 23:16.
[4] James 4:14.
[5] Ecclesiastes 1:14.
[6] Psalm 127:4.
[7] Deuteronomy 16:14.
[8] Moses Maimonides, *Mishneh Torah*, "Laws of the Festivals," 6:18.
[9] John 7:37.
[10] This outline for building a *sukkah* is modified from an article by Clarence Wagner, Jr., that appeared in *Restore!* (Vol. 5; No. 3) and was reprinted from *The Dispatch from Jerusalem*, official publication Jerusalem-based Bridges for Peace, Jerusalem.

A Sukkah (Hut) for the Feast of Tabernacles

Chapter 6

A Sanctuary of Blessing

HAVING A BLESSED HOME

Viewing the home as more than a domicile where families eat and sleep and watch television is the first step toward returning the home to its biblically Hebraic construct. The home is a sanctuary, a place for impartation of divine blessings that were initiated in the context of the family. The home is a blessed place, a sanctuary of blessing.

In the true spirit of divine blessing, what is blessed is to be a blessing. This is the case with the Sabbath, God's blessing that was always designed to be a blessing. *Shabbat* is a channel for divine blessing both in the home and in the community. The Jewish home is filled with the spirit of blessing throughout the Sabbath, which begins with a blessing and ends with a benediction. The blessing exercise of the Jewish family on the Sabbath is a great lesson for all believers. The principles can be employed in the context of the Christian family Sabbath.

A significant part of God's blessing for Abraham was this declaration: "In you all the families of the earth shall be blessed."[1] The specificity of the blessing was underscored by the transgenerational repetition of the same promise to Isaac: "In you and in your descendants all the families of the earth shall be blessed.[2] The repeated reference to families underscores God's ongoing blessing of the foundational unit of society, the family. The blessing that God gave to Abraham's family was to be extended to all the nations of the world, and the fundamental channel for the impartation of that blessing was to be the family.

A clear understanding of this truth was central to the Hebrew people who valued their families highly and maintained respect for parents, spouses, and children. The family was the unit for nurturing and strengthening individuals, as both husbands and wives profited from the balance of their relationship and children were nurtured in the security of a stable, loving environment and in the knowledge of the Lord. The home was a sanctuary of blessing.

THE CENTER FOR BLESSING

With the home viewed as not merely a secular social convention but as a holy place, the Hebraic family became a center for blessing. The divine imperative for blessing upon the children of Israel was fulfilled in the Jewish home. Parents assumed the role of priesthood to impart the blessing upon their children that God commanded: "This is the way you shall bless the children of Israel. . . ."[3] The blessing has been expanded to include other biblical elements and has become a much-anticipated weekly event in Jewish homes.

The prime importance that the Hebrews attached to domestic life was reinforced by the mutual respect that was maintained between parents and children. Children honored their parents even before it became a requirement of the Decalogue; therefore, they placed high value on the favor of their parents. This was especially true of parental blessings which both parents and children believed had profound power to produce good. In Hebrew culture, family blessings were highly prized, even considered the most valuable heritage that parents could bequeath to their children. The author of the apocryphal book of Ecclesiasticus observed that "a father's blessing gives a family firm roots."[4]

Blessing after Blessing

The vehicle that God chose for the impartation of his blessing to his children was the Sabbath. It has been said that Israel has not so much kept the Sabbath as the Sabbath has kept Israel. This has been especially true in the fact that the Sabbath is a family celebration. In the Christian world the one day in seven that has been set apart for God is viewed essentially as an opportunity for corporate worship. The Sabbath among the Jews, however, is first a family exercise that is then expanded into corporate worship. It is in the context of family intimacy that meeting, study, prayer, and blessing functions are fulfilled.

Like Abraham, the Sabbath was blessed so that it could be a blessing. It is a blessed time that sets apart a weekly occasion for blessing in the context of family and community. For millennia, therefore, millions of Jews have anxiously awaited *Shabbat* as the blessing that blesses. *Shabbat* begins on Friday evening at sundown and continues until Saturday evening.[5] In the Jewish home, the Sabbath is welcomed by the entire family, with the wife and daughters having received the honor of speaking the blessing and lighting the candles that usher in the Sabbath.

Spiritual exercises include reading God's Word, singing Psalms, and blessing children. The parents, with the father generally taking the leading role, place the blessing that God commanded for the children of Israel on each one of their own children individually. Because Jacob laid his right hand on Ephraim's head when he blessed him, the Jewish father lays his right hand on the head of each child as he speaks the blessing.[6] This blessing involves the combination of both the priestly benediction and other scriptural and personal blessings.

The blessing is introduced by statements that originate in classic biblical blessings. If the child is male, the words that Jacob commanded for the blessing are spoken: "In your name will Israel pronounce this blessing, 'May God make you like Ephraim and Manasseh.' "[7] If the child is female, the words of the blessing that the leaders of the Israelite community placed upon Ruth are added: "The Lord make you like Rachel and Leah, like Sarah and Rebecca."[8] Jewish girls are elevated in esteemed status to the rank of the women whom God used to establish the Hebrew people and the Israelite nation.

For both boys and girls, then, the blessing begins with the biblical declaration of benediction that was pronounced over their ancestors. These statements connect children with the ancient patriarchs and matriarchs of the faith, building their self-esteem and giving them a sense of context in their extended family community. It invokes importance and accomplishment into their young lives and sets expectations for their future.

After the initial benedictions, the process continues with the impartation of the blessing that God personally dictated to Moses and ordered to be spoken over all the children of Israel: "The Lord bless you and keep you. The Lord make his face shine upon you and be gracious unto you. The Lord lift up his countenance upon you and give you peace."[9] It may continue, "And they shall put my name upon the children of Israel, and I will bless them."[10]

Then, a personal blessing can speak good things into each child's life, including parental expectations and affirmation of the child's life ambition and the parents' commitment to assist in fulfilling that ambition. Other blessings may be added as well. This is in keeping with the tradition of Jacob who "blessed [his children], every one with the blessing appropriate to him."[11] This confirms more than a routine blessing by rote. It is a personalized blessing that recognizes accomplishment and speaks positive expectation into the life of each child.

The event can continue with the impartation of a request for the sevenfold Spirit of God to be upon each child: "May the Spirit of the Lord rest upon you, the spirit of wisdom, the spirit of understanding, the spirit of counsel, the spirit of might, the spirit of knowledge, and the spirit of the fear of the Lord."[12] Applying this blessing invokes the seven spirits that burn before God's throne[13] to be manifest in the child's life.

This practice of blessing children is a time-honored Jewish family exercise, part of a continuing emphasis on the value of blessing.[14] God commanded the blessing to be spoken over the children of Israel. Taking this instruction literally, parents bless their children. In the context of the extended family, teachers also bless their pupils.[15] The blessing was a family affair and a part of the community of extended family.

The second part of the family blessing features the husband blessing his wife by speaking, chanting, or singing in honor of his wife the Proverbs 31:10-31 benediction for the woman of valor: "What a rare find is a capable wife! Her worth is far beyond that of rubies . . . . Many women have done well, but you surpass them all." These words that "King Lemuel's"[16] mother taught him were declared in the scriptural record to be prophetic,[17] a fact that adds much weight to the blessing. The Jewish people believe that this blessing was originally spoken by Abraham in honor of Sarah and was subsequently transmitted orally through each generation. Whatever the case may be, speaking the Word of God in honor of one's wife is a powerful dynamic. It blesses her. It establishes her husband's high esteem for her in the eyes of their children. Perhaps even more important, it blesses the husband also, for he cannot repeat God's words of blessing without being impacted himself.

Before the meal, the father makes the *Kiddush* blessing, sanctifying the occasion by praising God for creating the fruit of the vine. A cup of wine is elevated, and these words are said: "Blessed are you, O Lord our God, King of the universe, who creates the fruit of the vine." All present then drink a portion of the wine. After the hands have been washed, the appropriate blessing is recited: "Blessed are you, O Lord our God, Ruler of the universe. You have sanctified us with your commandments and enjoined on us the cleansing of the hands." Then when all are seated, the father takes two specially prepared loaves of bread, elevates them, and makes this declaration: "Blessed are you, O Lord our God, King of the universe, who brings forth bread from the earth." Thereafter, everyone present eats a portion of the bread. Both the blessing for the wine and the blessing for the bread come from antiquity, predating the first century. Jesus spoke these blessings at the Last Supper.[18]

After the family shares a meal, the father leads in the offering of blessings to God after the meal called the *Birkat ha-Mazon.*[19] Of all the benedictions in Jewish ritual, it is considered to be the oldest and most important because it is the first blessing that God specifically commanded all of Israel to practice: "When you have eaten and are full, then you shall bless the Lord your God for the good land which he has given you."[20] In obedience to this instruction, the ancient Israelites prayed and blessed only after they had eaten, not before. In later times, however, the sages decided that blessings should be said before eating in the context of the belief that nothing should be enjoyed without first blessing God who made the provision.[21] The idea of blessing a meal before it is consumed is a Christian practice that is rooted more in the neo-Platonic idea that the material is evil and must be blessed. In history, it was also an attempt to pray over food that might be unhealthy or contain some toxin.

The *Birkat ha-Mazon* was originally comprised of three blessings: for food, for the land, and for Jerusalem. The blessing for food praises God for feeding all creatures, thereby connecting Israel with all living things. The blessing for the land expresses praise to God for the abundant land of Israel. The blessing for Jerusalem praises God as the "rebuilder" of Zion, thanks him for Jerusalem, and petitions his mercy for Israel. These three blessings predate the Christian era. A fourth blessing was added in the second century of the common era when the Jewish people were granted permission to bury their dead after the Romans crushed the revolt that had been led by messianic pretender Bar Kochba. It is a benediction of God who is "kindly and deals kindly with all."

The bestowing of blessings continues throughout the Sabbath, featuring both fellowship with family and worship with community. As the day comes to an end, the family again assembles for the *Havdalah* experience in which sorrow is expressed for the ending of the Sabbath and aromatic spices are used to carry the sweetness of the Sabbath over into the beginning of a new week.

The entire *Shabbat* experience is one of blessing after blessing. Blessings are imparted that strengthen the family bonds of mutual respect and honor. God is exalted in the context of the home, transforming it from a mere shelter from the elements into a spiritual sanctuary of safety and blessing. In the blessed home, Solomon's observation is true: "A righteous man who walks in his integrity–how blessed are his sons after him."[22]

The impact of family blessings such as these in Jewish homes is immeasurable. When recounting her childhood experiences of being blessed by her rabbi grandfather, Dr. Rachel Remen observed, "These few moments were the only time in my week when I felt completely safe and at rest."[23] If this were the only effect of the blessing, it would be reason enough for its impartation. The truth is, however, that the family blessings have life-giving and lifelong benefits.

SPECIAL BLESSING OCCASIONS

Significant events in the life cycle of each person are occasions for blessing. This is especially true in the development of a child. Blessing should begin with the time when conception has occurred to the end of the parent's allotted time on earth. Parents should never cease to bless their children.

Parents can speak words of blessing over the unborn child in its mother's womb. The blessing can petition divine protection and favor on both mother and child. Immediately after the birth of a child, parents can bless their newborn. In the Jewish community every son experiences the covenant of circumcision on the eighth day of his life. Christians can profit from this example by verbally blessing their infant children.

Parents have a significant opportunity to bless their children when they reach puberty and assume responsibility for their own actions. In Judaism, this experience is called *Bar Mitzvah* (son of the commandment). In many communities it is extended to girls as well in the *Bat Mitzvah* (daughter of the commandment). It is at the age of thirteen (twelve for girls) when the child comes of age. In the ceremony, the father publicly acknowledges that from this time forward he is no longer responsible for the child's actions. This is likely the source of the Christian idea of the "age of accountability," the age at which a child becomes responsible before God for his own actions.

This is a significant event, a rite of passage in the life of a young person. Christians can recognize this important time by publicly blessing their children and recognizing their transition from childhood and dependency on their parents to responsibility and maturity. A special blessing in addition to the weekly family *Shabbat* blessings can be spoken over the child to encourage the youngster at this rite of passage and affirm parental support as the child makes decisions for life.

One of the most important events in an individual's life is marriage, the making of a covenant with another person to join in unity and share life together. It is the time of the making of a new family, a new home. Parents should be carefully and prayerfully involved in this exercise. In ancient times, parents even chose mates for their children. Certainly parents should advise their children in what is one of life's most important decisions.

Then, children should want their parents to be involved in the ceremony that joins them covenantally with their mate. This is a significant opportunity for parents of both the bride and the groom to pronounce God's blessing and their own personal blessings over their children. The ceremony of marriage is enriched by the participation of parents in the one role that is assigned to them for life: blessing their children. The biblical blessing should be used, and additional blessings may be written into the liturgy for the event or may be given extemporaneously.

As children become adults, they have the privilege of continuing to receive their parents' blessings. There is never an age when they outgrow the blessing. At the same time, however, children have the opportunity to rise up and call their parents blessed,[24] to honor their father and mother[25] both in word and deed and to reciprocate the blessings that they have received from their parents by blessing them in turn.

When one reaches full age and is ready to be "gathered to his ancestors,"[26] this is an important time for the intimacy of the family to be manifest in blessing. A patriarch or matriarch will want to add God's blessing to children and grandchildren and to hear words of blessing from their most precious loved ones as they face the unknown but certain experience of death, burial, and resurrection.

Family blessing, then, is a lifetime affair. A blessed family never misses an opportunity for blessing one another. Family blessing is the heritage from the Lord, who is the source of all blessing that they experience in their family sanctuary.

BLESSING BY FAITH

Because Christians have not been accustomed to the biblical function of the home as the center for spiritual growth, they are often uncomfortable with assuming the role of leadership in blessing. Their codependency upon the clergy as the official channel of blessing has robbed them of this privilege. In many cases, the church has eviscerated the home of this, its most important function. Those who have come to realize the extent of their impoverishment through the loss of this important part of Christianity's Hebraic heritage can now reclaim their rights and privileges.

Generational inhibitions, however, can restrict the freedom to engage in what is clearly a parental responsibility. Because one's parents have not fulfilled this role is no excuse for not taking on the challenge. Because one is not fluent in verbal expression is also not an excuse. Perhaps what is needed is the faith to bless.

When discussing the subject of faith, most Christians' attention goes immediately to Hebrews 11, the one chapter in the Apostolic Scriptures that is often referred to as the "Hall of Fame of Faith." Here men and women of amazing faith are chronicled, along with some of the astounding results of their faith. There is Enoch who walked so closely with God that he was translated directly to God's presence so as not to experience death. There is Noah who built an ark and saved humanity from the deluge. There are Abraham and Sarah who, in their old age, experienced the miraculous birth of Isaac. There is Moses who delivered the Israelites from Egyptian bondage through astounding miracles. There are Gideon, Samson, David, and Samuel, all of whom witnessed supernatural intervention on behalf of the nation of Israel.

Two men are mentioned in this illustrious list, however, simply because they had the faith to bless their children and grandchildren: "*By faith* Isaac blessed Jacob and Esau in regard to their future . . . . *By faith* Jacob, when he was dying, blessed each of Joseph's sons"[27] (emphasis added). The faith that both Isaac and Jacob exhibited was equal to the faith that routed armies, divided the Reed Sea, preserved Noah's ark, and established prophets' words. It was faith that inspired these men to propel their values like arrows into the following generations in the form of blessings for their children and grandchildren.[28]

Should Christians who are filled with the Holy Spirit not have faith of the same caliber as that of Isaac and Jacob? Perhaps it is time to take the faith with which one believes to move mountains to begin with the blessing of children. It may seem like a leap of faith for some, but it is merely a step of obedience to God's command: "Bless the children of Israel." Without such a step of faith, one will experience the sorrow that Rachel Remen's mother noted when asked why she had not blessed her daughter: "I have blessed you every day of your life. . . . I just never had the wisdom to do it out loud."[29]

Fixed forms of blessing that the Jewish people have used for generations may be shared in the context of Christian families. Self-composed or spontaneous expressions may also be used. If nothing else, as a Christian, be Christlike: let it be said of you that you took your children up in your arms, "laid [your] hands on them, and blessed them,"[30] as Jesus did with the children who came to him. Whatever the case, by all means–and by faith–bless your children. Remember and follow the piety of King David, the man after God's own heart who, after dancing before the Ark of the Covenant with all his might, returned to the sanctuary of his own home so that he could bless his family.

OUTLINE FOR FAMILY BLESSINGS

When you as a Christian family gather together in your family sanctuary for the time set apart for God and family, you may wish to use the following outline as a guide for blessing both God and your family. This formula is similar to what has been done in Jewish homes for centuries. We have added language that expands the exercise to include various Christian elements.

Here is an example of Jewish fathers and grandfathers blessing their children under the covering of the *tallit* (the prayer shawl). The blessing may take many forms. You may even want to devise your own. The important thing is that you bless your children in your family sanctuary.

At sundown, the mother may light candles and make the following blessing:

"Blessed are you, O Lord our God, King of the universe, who has sanctified us by your Word and has called us to be a light unto our world. We thank you for your Son our Lord, Jesus the Christ, who has illuminated our lives with his divine presence and has given us eternal life."

The parents, with the father generally taking the leading role, now place the blessing that God commanded to be spoken over the children of Israel on each of their children. The priestly benediction is introduced by scriptural blessings appropriate to sons and daughters. Parents may lay their hands on the head of each child individually and make the following blessing:

"May the Lord make you like Ephraim and Manasseh" (if the child is a boy).

"May the Lord make you like Rachel and Leah, like Sarah and Rebecca" (if the child is a girl).

The blessing continues with this scripturally mandated personal blessing from God:

"The Lord bless you and keep you. The Lord make his face shine upon you and be gracious unto you. The Lord lift up his countenance upon you and give you peace."

You may continue:

"With this blessing, God said, 'I will put my name upon the children of Israel, and I will bless them.' "

Now, as Jacob did centuries ago, you should speak into each child's life a personal blessing that is appropriate to the child. This can express your praise for the child's accomplishment as well as your expectations for the child's future. This should amplify the child's vision and ambition for life.

The blessing can now continue with the invocation of the sevenfold Spirit of God upon the child:

"May the Spirit of God rest upon you, the spirit of wisdom, the spirit of understanding, the spirit of counsel, the spirit of might, the spirit of knowledge, and the spirit of the fear of the Lord. And may you always delight in the fear of the Lord."

Next, the husband blesses the wife by reading or reciting all or part of Proverbs 31:10-31:

"A wife of noble character who can find? She is worth far more than rubies. Her husband has full confidence in her and lacks nothing of value. She brings him good, not harm, all the days of her life. . . . She sets about her work vigorously . . . She opens her arms to the poor

and extends her hands to the needy. . . . Her husband is respected at the city gate, where he takes his seat among the elders of the land. . . . She speaks with wisdom, and faithful instruction is on her tongue. She watches over the affairs of her household and does not eat the bread of idleness. Her children arise and call her blessed; her husband also, and he praises her: 'Many women do noble things, but you surpass them all.' Charm is deceptive and beauty is fleeting; but a woman who fears the LORD is to be praised. Give her the reward she has earned, and let her works bring her praise at the city gate."

The wife may also bless her husband by reading or reciting Psalm 112:1-9:

"Blessed is the man who fears the LORD, who finds great delight in his commands. His children will be mighty in the land; the generation of the upright will be blessed. Wealth and riches are in his house, and his righteousness endures forever. Even in darkness light dawns for the upright, for the gracious and compassionate and righteous man. Good will come to him who is generous and lends freely, who conducts his affairs with justice. Surely he will never be shaken; a righteous man will be remembered forever. He will have no fear of bad news; his heart is steadfast, trusting in the LORD. His heart is secure, he will have no fear; in the end he will look in triumph on his foes. He has scattered abroad his gifts to the poor, his righteousness endures forever; his horn will be lifted high in honor."

Before the meal, the father takes a cup of grape juice or wine and makes the *Kiddush* blessing that Jesus and the apostles made:

"Blessed are you, O Lord our God, King of the universe, who has created the fruit of the vine." He may continue: *"We thank you for the blood of your Son that cleanses us from all iniquity."*

In like manner, the father takes two specially prepared loaves of bread and makes another blessing that Jesus made:

"Blessed are you, O Lord our God, King of the universe, who brings forth bread from the earth." He may continue: *"We thank you for your Son, the bread of life from heaven who strengthens our souls."*

The family shares a meal together at which there may be singing and sharing of God's Word. In the course of the meal, they may discuss the significance of the foods on the table that date from Bible times: bread, wine, oil, and salt, all of which have great spiritual significance.

When the meal is concluded, the family may join in blessing God for the foods. This is in obedience to God's command that the children of Israel were to bless the Lord after they had eaten and were full.[31] The following *Birkhat ha-Mazon* blessing dates from before the time of Jesus:

The father says: *"Let us say grace."* The rest of the family responds: *"Blessed be the Name of the Lord from this time forth and for ever."* The father continues: *"We will bless him of whose bounty we have partaken."* The family responds: *"Blessed be he of whose bounty we have partaken and through whose goodness we live."*

The family together may say all or part of the following blessing:

"Blessed are you, O Lord our God, King of the universe, who feeds the whole world with your goodness, with grace, with loving kindness and tender mercy; you give food to all flesh, for your loving kindness endures for ever. Through your great goodness we have never lacked food: O may we never lack it for ever and ever for your great Name's sake, since you nourish and sustain all beings, and do good unto all, and provide food for all your creatures whom you have created. Blessed are you, O Lord, who gives food to all.

"We thank you, O Lord our God, because you gave

as an heritage unto our fathers a desirable, good, and ample land . . . and for the food wherewith you do constantly feed and sustain us on every day, in every season, at every hour. For all this, O Lord our God, we thank and bless you. Blessed be your Name by the mouth of all living continually and for ever, even as it is written, And you shall eat and be satisfied, and you shall bless the Lord your God for the good land which he has given you. Blessed are you, O Lord, for the land and for the food.

"Have mercy, O Lord our God, upon Israel your people, upon Jerusalem your city, upon Zion the abiding place of your glory, upon the kingdom of the house of David, and upon the great and holy house that was called by your Name. O Lord our God, our Father, feed us, nourish us, sustain, support and relieve us, and speedily, O Lord our God, grant us relief from all our troubles. We beseech you, O Lord our God, let us not be in need either of the gifts of mortals or of their loans, but only of your helping hand, which is full, open, holy, and ample, so that we may never be put to shame or humiliated. And rebuild Jerusalem the holy city speedily in our days. Blessed are you, O Lord, who in your compassion rebuilds Jerusalem. Amen."

The family may conclude by praying the Lord's Prayer, after which the father may say, *"Now, may the grace of our Lord Jesus Christ, the love of God, and the fellowship of the Holy Spirit be with us all. Amen."*

This concludes the *erev Shabbat* (Sabbath evening) family blessing exercise.

OUTLINE FOR BLESSING A CHILD AT PUBERTY

In addition to the usual *Shabbat* blessing for children, you may say, *"We bless you in the name of the Lord as you make this important transition in life. May you ever hide God's Word in your heart so you do not sin against him. As you now take responsibility for your own actions before God, we will stand with you and assist you in fulfilling your vision for life. May you ever live in the richest of God's blessings."*

OUTLINE FOR A WEDDING BLESSING

You may say these words over your daughter, "*We bless you in the name of the Lord. You have been God's gift in our lives, and we rejoice that you are now giving yourself in love to make a new family. A wife of valor is priceless . . . many women have done noble things, but you excel them all, for a woman who fears the Lord shall be praised.*[32] *May you be like Rachel and Leah, like Sarah and Rebecca. The Lord bless you and keep you. The Lord cause his face to shine upon you and be gracious unto you. The Lord turn his face toward you and give you peace. May you and your beloved ever live in the richest of God's blessings."*

You may say these words over your son, "*We bless you in the name of the Lord. You have been God's gift in our lives, and we rejoice that you are now giving yourself in love to make a new family. The husband who fears the Lord will be lifted high in honor. You are a gracious, compassionate, and righteous man; therefore, your generation will be blessed.*[33] *May you be like Ephraim and Manasseh. The Lord bless you and keep you. The Lord cause his face to shine upon you and be gracious unto you. The Lord turn his face toward you and give you peace. May you and your beloved ever live in the richest of God's blessings."*

[1] Genesis 12:3, New Revised Standard Version.
[2] Genesis 28:14, New American Standard Version.
[3] Numbers 6:23.
[4] Ecclesiasticus (Sirach) 3:9.

[5] In biblical terms, the day begins at sundown so that evening precedes morning and a day is defined as "evening and morning," even as the biblical creation narrative declares (cf. Genesis 1:5).

[6] Genesis 48:17.

[7] Genesis 48:20.

[8] Ruth 4:11.

[9] Numbers 6:23-26.

[10] Numbers 6:27.

[11] Genesis 49:28, New American Standard Version.

[12] Isaiah 11:1-3.

[13] Revelation 4:5.

[14] It is uncertain how ancient the Jewish practice of blessing children may be. Its earliest mention in extant literature is in *Brautspiegel*, a book published in Basel in 1602. The writer stresses the fact that children should be trained from infancy to value parental blessings: "Before the children can walk they should be carried on Sabbath and holidays to the father and mother to be blessed; after they are able to walk they shall go of their own accord with bowed body and shall incline their heads and receive the blessing." See Moses Henochs, *Brautspiegel*, quoted in "Blessing of Children," Jewish Encyclopedia.com. p. 3.

[15] In *Synagoga Judaica*, published in 1604, Buxtorf notes that on Sabbath parents bless their children and teachers bless their pupils.

[16] It is thought that Lemuel may well have been a term of endearment for Solomon himself.

[17] Proverbs 31:1.

[18] Matthew 26:26-27.

[19] *Mazon* means "foods."

[20] Deuteronomy 8:10.

[21] Babylonian Talmud, *Berakoth* 35a.

[22] Proverbs 20:7, New American Standard Version.

[23] Rachel Naomi Remen, *My Grandfather's Blessing* (New York: Riverdale Books, 2002), p. 48.

[24] Proverbs 31:28.

[25] Exodus 20:12.

[26] Genesis 49:29.

[27] Hebrews 11:20-21.

[28] Psalm 127:4.

[29] Rachel Naomi Remen, p. 88.

[30] Mark 10:16.

[31] Deuteronomy 8:10.

[32] These words are taken from Proverbs 31:10ff.

[33] These words are taken from Psalm 112.

Chapter 7

Family Halachah

Establishing Secure Borders

Halachah is a very important term in Judaism and among the Jewish people. Taken from the Hebrew word הָלַךְ (*halak*, meaning "to walk"), it describes the established norm for right conduct in a community. It literally means "a prescribed manner of living" and is used to define the Jewish lifestyle. Generally, *halachah* is an outline of standards for human actions in specific situations that have been determined by the spiritual leaders of Jewish communities. These findings are based on rabbinic interpretation of both the Torah (the Pentateuch) and oral tradition (called the "oral torah") which has been codified in the Talmud (composed of commentaries upon the Torah called the *Mishnah* and commentaries on the *Mishnah* called the *Gemara*). *Halachah*, then, is an effort to provide guidelines for roles and boundaries for Jewish individuals, for Jewish families, and for Jewish communities. *Halachah* defines what is required to be a member in good standing of the Jewish community and a practitioner of Judaism.

Roles for men, women, and children are specifically defined in this monumental corpus of literature that was developed through centuries of dialogue, disputation, and formulation. Likewise, boundaries are established within which Jewish people can function without fear of violating the Torah's instructions. The Talmud has been highly valued because it has been a boundary-defining mechanism that has constructed a "fence around the Torah," warning of impending violation of God's commandments if one ventures beyond its borders.

Christian families can well profit from understanding the principle of *halachah* used in the Jewish community. First, the church in its various communions should (and does) define roles for men, women, and children and for leaders and communicants in the community of faith. These leadership entities should also define what is considered acceptable conduct within the communities. At the same time, however, the *halachah* principle should also be manifest in the home, so that each family, within the guidelines of its constituent community, determines standards for acceptable conduct within the home. Boundaries are secure borders that limit the incursion of damaging forces into the safety of the family sanctuary.

CONFUSION AND REMOVED PERIMETERS

In modern society, secularism and atheism have purposely blurred both roles and boundaries for human interpersonal relationships, especially as they relate to the home. It is increasingly important, therefore, that Christian families assume their God-given responsibility to function within the context of the roles that God has established for husbands, wives, fathers, mothers, and children. Christian families must also establish and maintain boundaries for what is considered proper ethical and social conduct in their homes. Going with the societal flow down the broad road will lead to disintegration and destruction of the most precious earthly thing that believers have, their family relationships.

The atheistic secular mind has purposely sought to confuse masculine and feminine roles, all in the name of liberating women. At the same time, it has carefully and systematically inculcated the concepts of consequentialism or situational ethics, which fundamentally are no ethics at all, for absolutes are not recognized. Generations of children have been reared (actually "raised" like soybeans or corn) in an environment lacking clear gender role models and void of the moral compass of absolutes ethics. This violence against the body politic of society has crept with treacherous subtlety into the church and synagogue, corrupting the thinking of both of the communities that have been commissioned to be God's light to the world.

The overwhelming onslaught of political correctness has demanded that everyone in society conform to its demand for the homogenization of society and the destruction of antiquated mores. All of this has been very subtly introduced in the name of tolerance. "I'm ok, you're ok," and "I have my truth; you have your truth," are the mantras of political correctness. Christians have been swept along in this tide of deceit and perversion, compromising the fundamental concepts of their faith in a drive toward being seen as tolerant and accommodating.

The result is that in Christian homes, the divorce rate is as great as or greater than that of society in general. Christian men and women no longer have a clear sense of self-identity and purpose. They do not understand their roles. They no longer insist on biblical morality, allowing their standards to be set by the entertainment industry through the ubiquitous television and all-pervasive music. If a popular movie or music idol does something, it must not be all that bad. "Have we just been too old fashioned?" parents wonder. "After all, God *is* love." Someone has observed that as a result of this kind of mentality, "the church has become so worldly and the world has become so churchy that it is increasingly difficult to tell the difference."

What are parents who have not been totally blinded by societal attacks upon their roles and boundaries to do? The answer is a "back-to-the-Bible" movement. The old book that everyone thought was outdated myth is the answer, the most up-to-date manual for human behavior that exists in the world. When believers return to the Holy Scriptures they find the answers. It is far more important and of eternal consequence to be biblically correct than it is to be politically correct.

In order for the Bible to be rightly applied, however, it must be interpreted in the light of the culture and history of the people to whom, through whom, and for whom it was given. The Bible is a Jewish book and can be understood only with a Jewish mindset and worldview. Interpreting Holy Scripture through the lenses of cultures that are foreign to the book and its fundamental premises has resulted in perverted teachings that have produced the opposite of biblical intent. It is from these aberrant religious concepts that societies have sought relief, swinging the conceptual pendulum to opposite extremes of total secularization.

Redefining biblically Hebraic roles for family members could never be more important than at this time. Likewise, establishing clear biblical boundaries for ethical conduct and proper interpersonal relationships could never be more essential than now. In the face of the subtle satanic attack on the very foundation of society's social fabric, it is important that Christians return to doing God's thing God's way. To do less or more is to invite further disintegration of the family.

BIBLICAL ROLES

Despite secularist efforts to encourage a unisex view of humanity, there is a difference! Masculinity is masculinity, and femininity is femininity. Men are men, and women are women. Attempts by sociological revisionism to blur psychological lines by insisting that men discover their feminine side and women assert their masculine side have not resulted in the emergence of a physical androgyne, the perfect hermaphrodite. If there is no difference between male and female, why are millions of dollars spent annually on sonograms in order to determine as early as possible the gender of a fetus? And, why at a baby's birth are its genitalia the first anatomical parts that are examined so that its gender can be confirmed? Yes, there is a physical difference, and there are mental, psychological, and emotional differences as well. These differences are in no way demeaning to either male or female, nor do they make either lesser than or subject to the other. They are simply differences that God intended to be complementary and balancing.

When either males or females are forced to develop their self-identities in what they are not, turmoil results. When men are forced into feminine roles and women are forced into masculine roles, confusion breeds uncertainty and emotional instability. Male and female acceptance of biblical roles establishes healthy foundations for joyful, successful living and brings honor to God. Since personality can only reveal itself in persons, it is "specifically in human nature–in man and woman–that we see God."[1] When husbands determine to be fully male and wives determine to be fully female within the context of gender-role parameters established in the Holy Scriptures, marriage and family are strengthened by the divinely ordained counterbalance that is holistic and healthy.

Roles, like boundaries, can only be worked out in detail in the context of community and the home. No specific blueprint for human personality can be forced upon each individual. Even in discussing biblical roles, one can only speak in generalities and of norms. Each individual is different and will find fulfillment only in a personalized and contextualized manifestation of the general principles that the Scriptures describe. This process is the same for cultural applications of biblical concepts in the larger communities of faith. Divine principles may not be compromised or syncretized with human or satanic ideas; however, they must be contextualized in the indigenous cultures in which they are manifest. Otherwise, individuals and groups are being required to be what they are not.

Various personality types will interrelate in different ways in marriage and family. This underscores the importance of communicating and establishing realistic expectations both for roles and boundaries in each individual marriage and family. Extroverts, introverts, and ambiverts will relate to one another in different manners and to varying degrees. Analytical, driver, amiable, and expressive personality types will relate to one another in various ways. Some are born or trained leaders; others are followers. Most are somewhere in between. It is important, therefore, that each community and ultimately each family work out its own roles and boundaries within the context of biblically Hebraic guidelines.

BIBLICALLY HEBRAIC MARRIAGE

Marriage is perhaps one of the least understood institutions in today's world. This most intimate of interpersonal relationships has been grounded more in the ideas of pagan philosophers than in the teaching of Hebrew prophets and apostles. The results could hardly be more disastrous for the well being of society. In order to put things right in the understanding of the home, it is important to begin with the institution that creates a home in the first place. Marriage must be returned to the biblically Hebraic matrix from which it emerged.

Marriage was instituted by God himself in Eden. It was the divine design for human companionship and for the perpetuation of the human species. God joined Adam and Eve together as one and commanded that all subsequent human beings find their mate and be likewise joined in marital congress. Marriage is the process of reuniting separated male and female genders into one superentity. It is a return to the wholeness of oneness. It is the fulfillment of the divine command that children leave their parents and become joined together in covenantal unity[2] so that they can fulfill the first divine injunction: "Be fruitful and multiply and fill the earth.[3] Erasmus declared, "Much reverence is due [marriage] which was instituted by God [before all else]. The rest were instituted upon earth, but this in paradise. The rest for a remedy, this for partnership in happiness."[4]

Marriage has always been the legitimate order for human intimacy and procreation. Those who would join themselves together physically must first engage in a covenantal relationship, a lifelong commitment to fidelity. The form and order of this agreement may vary widely; however, the divine principle of covenant is inviolable. Any consummation of intimacy outside this boundary is illegitimate and sinful, the violation of divine commandments.[5]

By making a marriage covenant before God, husband and wife create a holy sanctuary in which they are privileged to share in God's creative work, sustaining life and making it holy. The traditional marriage ceremony in Judaism features the exchange of a ring(s) and the declaration: "Behold, you are consecrated unto me by this ring." Christian weddings feature similar words that create a state of holiness (separation) in which life can be wholly embraced. For the couple who are thus consecrated to one another, the rest of humanity disappears, forsaken for the sanctity of their union in their family sanctuary.

God expressed his concern that his children respect the sanctity of marriage when he declared, "the wife of your youth . . . is your partner, the wife of your marriage covenant. Has not the LORD made them one? In flesh and spirit they are his. And why one? Because he was seeking a godly offspring. So guard yourself in your spirit, and do not break faith with the wife of your youth."[6] As far as God is concerned, marriage is far more than a mere social convention. It is a sacred commitment, the foundation of the home and of society. It is a divinely sanctioned state of oneness that can be paralleled only in the unity that exists in God himself. The divine rationale for this oneness was that "godly offspring" might be produced and subsequently nurtured in the admonition of the Lord.[7] Is it any wonder, then, that it has been asserted that marriage has always been the instrument of the survival of the Jewish people and of the preservation of its faith.[8]

God's design for marriage is inherently monogamous, with one man and one woman joined together first covenantally and then physically. This is clear from the first marriage. Polygamy is an aberration, a departure from God's design.[9] Divorce, though permitted because of the hardness of men's hearts, was never God's intention for his human creation. Jesus observed that "from the beginning it was not so,"[10] and he commanded that what God has joined together man should not put asunder.[11] Divorce may be necessary because of infidelity, abuse, neglect, or hardness of heart. Remarriage also receives divine sanction in certain circumstances.[12] Neither divorce or remarriage is preferred, however, because when they occur, God's original intent for human marriage in Eden has not been fulfilled.[13]

The ideal must be the goal of every person and every marriage; however, the real condition of sinful humanity frequently falls short of the ideal. The reason that ancient Israel accepted divorce and remarriage was for the protection of the innocent victims of those who sinned against God and against covenanted married partners. Judaism's focus on social justice has been manifest first in society's most fundamental unit where the right to divorce and remarriage has been upheld in situations of spousal abuse and neglect.

Dysfunctional individuals and families in the modern world result from failure to follow God's instructions for human behavior. Men and women today, like their counterparts in all previous generations, have chosen to follow human perspectives on interpersonal relations rather than God's instructions. The result, as always, is disaster. It would profit all believers to review pagan concepts of marriage and compare them with biblical instructions to see which options more significantly influence their thinking and their lives.

In much of the ancient world, marriage was a mere

social convention, a means of ensuring that a man could have some degree of certainty that his children and heirs were his own flesh and blood. In Greece and Rome, sexual and social pleasures were taken in the temples of the gods and in the company of prostitutes and courtesans, an accepted societal norm. Wives were kept cloistered in the home, almost under lock and key, especially in Greece, where it was considered disgraceful for a wife to be seen in a public place without her husband. Demosthenes said, "Mistresses we keep for pleasure . . . wives are to bear us legitimate children."[14]

The predominant idea of love in these societies was based in eroticism. Men and women were always falling in love, victims of Cupid's arrows. This erotic kind of love, however, is not a sound basis for founding a home, for it is inherently selfish, borne out of the quest to satisfy individual desires for pleasure. This love lust is grounded in self-gratification and self-fulfillment. Partners, like Tristan and Isolde of Arthurian legend, are madly and hopelessly in love; however, their experience is really a mutual narcissism, a self love of passion-generated vision of the perfect lover.[15]

True love is an outworking of marriage. While physical attraction is important in this most intimate of relationships, marriages that are founded solely on erotic impulses are often doomed to failure because the sacrificing of the individual self in order to maintain and strengthen the greater whole is not its driving impulse. Usually, erotic lovers are more in love with themselves than they are with their partners and are focused on fulfilling their own emotional needs and hormonal impulses.

Biblical marriage is based primarily on covenantal commitment to God and to one's spouse first, and only secondarily on love second. The sages have suggested that this truth is illustrated in the fact that Isaac "took Rebekah, and she became his wife; and he loved her,"[16] in that order. Only when it is nurtured in a close domestic setting can love become a permanent foundation for a home. Love is an essential ingredient for successful marriage, but it is a love that is considerate of the needs and desires of one's partner. It is a self-sacrificing love similar to that with which Christ loved the church.[17] This kind of love will focus attention on one's spouse, seeing that the partner's needs and desires are fulfilled. It confirms the view that the two are actually one and that pleasuring one's spouse is pleasuring oneself. When both partners love one another unselfishly, both receive more than they give. True love produces satisfaction for the giver in the fulfillment of the spouse's needs and desires.

Marital love is not a Platonic experience that has as its ideal an escape from physical contact and pleasure. Christian theologians through the centuries have postulated that the "original sin" in Eden was sexual congress and that sin is propagated from generation to generation through the "concupiscence of sexual relations."[18] The ideal for much of Christianity has been total abstinence from sexual intercourse either through celibacy or through overcoming the desire for physical intimacy in marriage except for the express purpose of procreation. Tertullian expressed clerical disdain for intimacy in marriage this way: "Between marriage and fornication there is a legal, but not an intrinsic difference."[19]

Sexual intercourse is a central element in biblical marriage. Whereas many Christian teachers have considered marital intercourse on Sunday to be sinful, the Jewish understanding is that coital engagement on Sabbath is the performance of a *mitzvah* (a commandment or good deed) and is blessed of God. The truth is that God created both human genitalia and sexual desire and said both were good. Then he specifically commanded the physical joining of husband and wife in marriage so that those desires would be fulfilled.

As a Jewish teacher, Paul understood this biblically Hebraic truth. He declared: "But since there is so much immorality, each man should have his own wife, and each woman her own husband. The husband should fulfill his marital duty to his wife, and likewise the wife to her husband. The wife's body does not belong to her alone but also to her husband. In the same way, the husband's body does not belong to him alone but also to his wife. Do not deprive each other."[20] Though the subsequent church had much difficulty understanding and accepting it, the Apostle to the Gentiles readily understood this biblically Hebraic truth and accurately represented it.

Somehow the church has been ashamed to talk about what God was not ashamed to create. In its often smug self-righteousness and hyper-holiness, the church has considered inherently evil and dirty what God called good at the moment of its creation. From a Hebraic perspective, all human organs are entirely neutral, and all can be used both for good or evil.[21] Anatomical parts serve various functions; however, none is evil *per se* or more inclined toward evil. Acts of intimacy in marriage, therefore, are far from evil. Indeed, they are blessed of God when they are carried out in mutual love and respect. The Scriptures command it: "Rejoice with the wife of your youth. Let her breasts satisfy thee at all times; and be thou ravished always with her love."[22]

Intercourse is the glue of biblical marriage. It is the literal fulfillment of the biblical commandment to "cleave" (be glued together).[23] While it also serves the physical function of procreation, its principal purpose is companionship and intimacy, bonding and renewing by entwined physical bodies the spiritual connectivity of the marriage covenant. This experience brings wholeness to both husband and wife, both of whom are designed by God to experience the ecstasy of orgasmic fulfillment.

Much of Christianity has propounded the myth of female asexuality. Indeed, until the twentieth century, the mere suggestion that a woman could have a desire for sexual fulfillment or could experience sexual pleasure would have been viewed as "casting vile aspersions on womankind."[24] Many have insisted that only women of depraved morality can experience either physical or emotional satisfaction from sexual intercourse. Wives merely serve as receptacles for their husbands' passions in this perverted thinking. The biblically Hebraic truth is that God created female sexuality and empowered the female both physically and emotionally with the capacity for complete sexual gratification. As a matter of fact, in Jewish tradition a wife is encouraged to take the initiative in helping her husband fulfill her conjugal needs.[25]

From a biblically Hebraic perspective, not only is a wife expected to have sexual desires, but her husband is required to bring her sexual satisfaction. This idea is based on the commandment that prohibits a husband from going to war or being engaged in any business for one year after marriage so that may remain at home and "bring happiness" to his bride.[26] The Hebrew word translated "bring happiness" is שָׂמַח (*samach*) and has been interpreted by the sages of Israel to include a requirement that a husband bring his wife complete sexual gratification. In Jewish understanding sex is a wife's right and a husband's duty,[27] not vice versa as it has been perceived in much of the Gentile world. The Talmud declares that a man who "neglects his marital duties to his wife is a sinner,"[28] and it also teaches that a husband who ensures that his wife attains orgasm before he does is rewarded.[29] While any form of physical intimacy that brings pleasure to both husband and wife is acceptable,[30] sexual compulsion in any form is condemned in Jewish law.[31]

The ideal of marriage is one of mutual submission. Even the scriptural injunction for wives to submit to their husbands is prefaced by the command: "Submit yourselves one to another out of reverence for Christ."[32] Marital partners exhibit mutual respect and deference to one another out of honor for the Messiah. The superentity that they have formed through covenantal fusion transcends their individuality. The oneness they have achieved supersedes everything that they could have been as individuals. Both husband and wife see this entity manifest in their life partner. When martial partners function together equally, with distinct, though equivalent roles, the exponential effect can be truly godly; however, if the hubris of one induces an attempt to dominate the other, the potentially divine effect is canceled, stultified, and silenced.[33]

Mutual submission means maintaining communication and receiving a mate's counsel. Abraham was commanded of God, "Listen to whatever Sarah tells you," when questions about Hagar and Ishmael arose.[34] It is through such acts of mutual support that the Jewish ideal of *shalom bayit* (peace in the home) is maintained. Creating and maintaining *shalom bayit* is viewed as a sacred trust and a holy task among the Jewish people. Peace in the home is the foundation of peace in the community and ultimately in the world.

Without the sanctity of marriage, there can never be sanctity in the home. The quality of family life can only be as good as the quality of marital harmony, and marital harmony can only be attained when each partner recognizes God first, spouse second, and self last. A solid, God-centered marriage that is grounded in solidly biblical principles is the foundation of the family sanctuary.

BIBLICALLY HEBRAIC MANHOOD

So many diverse opinions on the role of men in the home and society have been projected in the modern world that most men simply do not know what is expected of them or what to expect of themselves. From the chauvinism of the past, to the machismo of some cultures, to the chivalry of others, to demands for a unisex view of humanity–a wide range of ideas has been promoted for true masculinity. Reacting to millennia of abusive treatment of women in male-dominated societies, militant feminism has sought to redefine masculine roles. Some have projected the idea that women are superior to men, that all men are pigs, and that men serve only one function–the perpetuation of the species. Others suggest that men should somehow get in touch with their feminine side. With all of these diverse expectations, men today don't know whether to flex their muscles or cry!

This confusion has produced a dilemma of self-identity and self-worth for many, if not most, males in today's society. While the situation has produced a healthy rethinking of male abuses in the past, the problem is that the reevaluation process has failed to return to the one source where accurate and workable information can be found about masculine roles. The Bible has been viewed as either having contributed to the problem or having been its outright source, not its solution. Differing ideas of masculinity have been projected from a perceptive and reactive basis rather than from an apperceptive and proactive stance. Perceived evils of the past have brought reactions in the present. This approach to historical problems, however, often creates an equally destructive "solution." What is needed is an apperceptive approach of purposely returning to the original models to arrive at a healthy, productive understanding. Then, proactive measures can be taken to restore those foundations, contextualized for the diverse manifestations of society in the world today. The answer is a return to the biblically Hebraic models for manhood.

In most ways, men and women are alike, if not identical. Genetically, less than one per cent of human composition differs between male and female. This should stress the absolute equality of men and women in their humanity and underscore the fact that neither should dominate the other. There are, however, distinct differences, and these differences occur in very important areas of life. The anatomical differences are obvious even to the most strident of militant unisexists; however, there are also psychological, emotional, and spiritual differences. Differences, however, can only be projected as generalizations, not as absolutes that can be applied in every individual. They are manifest in categories of understanding and principles of application, none of which is an absolute law to which there are no exceptions.

One of the roles of manhood was established in God's declaration to the first man following the fall: "In the sweat of your face you will eat bread."[35] It is specific, though not unique to manhood that God has designated males as providers. For this reason, males tend to be more adventurous, self-assertive, and competitive. They generally take more chances even from childhood. Males tend to think more logically and clinically; therefore, in childhood they generally manifest greater interest in and aptitude for math and science skills than their female counterparts. Males also tend to be less in touch with their emotions and generally are less creative. Their thinking is essentially left-brain dominated, differing from females whose brain hemispheres are more directly connected so that they also think spatially and with block logic.

God's pronouncement regarding Adam was not a curse. It was a recognition that his post-fall role would continue the function that he had had from the beginning when he was commissioned to be a keeper of the garden.[36] The rigors would be expanded because of sin; however, the role remained the same. For this reason, males have always established much of their self-identity in their work. Men are defined by what they do. This is good in that inbred in man is a work ethic that promotes the survival and welfare of the human race. It can be bad, however, when men get out of balance with their work-defined self-image. Workaholic lifestyles can debilitate both men and their families.

Unlike females, men are not relationally defined; therefore, it is easy for them to be detached and clinical, giving little thought to the interpersonal interaction that is necessary for healthy families. For men, it is not "who you are," but "what you do." For this reason, males tend to be more ego-oriented than females. As a result, they need affirmation, not negation. They need a sense of worth; however, their self-worth is not measured by who they are, but by what they do. Men are by definition doers. It is a part of their role as providers.

An outworking of this role is the male tendency to "take charge," to rule. Indeed, in the beginning, humankind was given the right to rule over the rest of creation. After the fall, this responsibility was specifically placed upon the man who was told that he would rule over the woman and that the woman would relate to her husband in a complementary role. The Edenic ideal was for the man to serve as protector and provider and the woman to serve as a nurturer and balance to the man. Sin, however, has extrapolated those functions into a twisted form of co-dependency in which men have been abusively dominant and women have been pressured into submission beyond reason or divine intent. Spousal abuse has, therefore, generally been a male phenomenon, an outworking of sin in the most fundamental of human relationships.

There is, however, a need for someone to take charge, especially in times of impending danger. God has designed the male spirit to rise up and meet a challenge head on; however, he has balanced that tendency with the caution and care of the female personality. If this balance had not been in place, males would have destroyed the earth long ago with their reckless adventurism. Again, these generalizations are not absolutes, for there are men who are less driven, and there are women who are bold and adventurous. The generalizations, however, reflect the divine intent in the way in which God structured male and female in every aspect of their existence.

The role of manhood in the family is clearly established in the first of the three blessings in the Aaronic benediction. This tripartite blessing can be seen as coming from the Father, the Son, and the Holy Spirit. The first blessing is from the Father: "The LORD bless you and keep you."[37] It is uniquely the function of fatherhood to "bless and keep." Blessing and keeping involve reordering the natural instinct toward self-interest to think of others, specifically one's spouse and children.

Blessing and keeping also require work, man's defining activity. Without work, men have low self-esteem. Government programs that promote indolence and laziness are debilitating to men. Men who do not work are not fulfilling the most basic of instructions for masculinity: "In the sweat of your face you will eat bread."[38] They are not fulfilling their commission to bless and keep their families. Nothing could be more devastating to the male sense of self-worth than the failure to fulfill the responsibilities assigned to him by God.

Work becomes more than an exercise of toil and suffering when it is understood from a biblically Hebraic perspective. Work is worship, and every man's work is a ministry. These ideas sound entirely alien to traditional Christian understanding, for the church has projected the idea that only clergymen do "God's work," making all other labor purely secular and carnal.

The bifurcation of life into two hemispheres, the spiritual and the secular, has been one of the most debilitating devices that Satan has used against the health of the church and its fundamental unit, the family. As a result, some men's work has been demeaned while that of others has been elevated to a lofty status. Since their work has not been considered to be spiritual, most males have found very little of their self-identity in the spiritual matters of the church. They have viewed themselves in a secularist perspective, making it easier to escape responsibility for spiritual matters in their own homes and in the church. It has also set them up in opposition to the church's spiritual leaders, forcing them to vie with polished, professional "men of God" for attention and respect in their families.

By removing the work that man is inherently driven to do from the neo-Platonic sphere of the material and secular and returning it to the realm of the spiritual as an act of worship, the biblically Hebraic understanding places work in the right context and elevates male self-worth to its God-given perspective. There is no difference of value between any work, for it is all spiritual, not carnal. Man's work is an act of obedience to God's command both in Eden[39] and in the Sinai proclamation: "Six days you shall work."[40] This view causes every man to understand that he has a ministry: the work to which God has called him. It also underscores to him the importance of maintaining spiritual standards in every aspect of his life, not just those few moments when he is "in church." Viewing his work as his ministry gives every man a sense of its importance in the eyes of God and places a weight of responsibility on his shoulders to do justice and love mercy in the marketplace and in the home.

The male composition is also defined in leadership. While all men are not leaders, the rule of thumb for masculinity has been a tendency to step up and take the lead. This again is a God-given, innate characteristic that is essential for human well-being. The most important place for man to lead is in the home. This leading must be from a godly perspective of servant leadership. Otherwise, sin will transform God's good intention into a twisted and evil distortion of abusive relationships.

A godly man will take the initiative to lead his family in every aspect of life. His servant leadership will facilitate physical, social, and psychological development of every family member. He will lead by example, not by fiat. He will be lord of his home because he acts like the Lord of heaven in sacrificing his own needs and wants for the welfare of his family. Jesus set the example of familial love in giving himself for the church, his bride.[41] The Father also gave his only begotten Son to redeem his children from their sins.[42] There is no sacrifice that is too great for servant leaders in godly homes.

The first sphere where husbands and fathers should lead their families is in social interaction. This is an area where men need a lot of help. They tend not to be relational. They are usually laconic and are generally deficient in verbal expression. Their conversation skills are often underdeveloped. First, most men suffer from an attention deficit syndrome: they just don't listen, and they don't want to linger in a conversation or discussion so that understanding or clarification is achieved. Proof of this is seen in male domination of remote control devices and their ability to view multiple television programs simultaneously. Since women are more expressive, especially in verbal articulation, they have a biological need to talk, and they need someone to hear them, particularly their spouses. Women need to bring this balance of ability and attention to the home and help their spouses meet this need for social interaction for the health of the family.

Leading in familial social interaction takes commitment and time, both of which are often deficient in men. In order to lead, however, men must take the initiative and lead by example. They need to learn to listen creatively, to foster an environment in the home that is conducive to dialogue and communication. They need to learn to initiate the interaction if they are to be true servant leaders, standing out front and pointing the way through their own actions.

The second area where husbands and fathers should also lead is in study. Every Jewish father has the responsibility of leading his family in two areas of study. First, he must teach his children the Torah or the Word of God. Second, he must teach his children a means of livelihood. All successful homes must feature these two levels of teaching. Men must take the time to educate themselves in God's Word so that they can teach divine truths in the context of their families and not leave that responsibility to Sunday Schools and other church programs. Specific times must be allotted on the family calendar for just such educational efforts.

In order to "bless and keep" his family, a father must also either teach and mentor his children in job skills, or he must provide a plan of education that will inculcate those skills so that each child can have the knowledge and experience to be successful in the role and work to which he or she has been called. A wise father is one who recognizes early in a child's life the predispositions that the child has and then nurtures that child in the achievement of life ambitions.

Leading in teaching must be in the context of the ancient Hebraic model for the transfer of knowledge: "Come, walk the road with me." This was the methodology of the sages who understood that they taught better by example. As their disciples followed them down the road, they taught them from the life situations that they encountered. They conveyed understanding in what they did, so that their disciples imitated their lifestyle.

This is the very essence of Christian discipleship that must begin in the home. Jesus invited his disciples to follow him[43] and Paul encouraged believers to be followers of him as he followed Christ.[44] Learning is best acquired, therefore, by modeling the actions of leaders. Indeed, the Greek word Paul uses for "followers" is μιμητής (*mimetes*), which literally means "to imitate" and is the etymological derivation of the English words *mime* and *mimicry*.

In fact, this is what children do anyway. They imitate their parents, either for good or bad. Following in father's or mother's footsteps is perfectly natural for little children. In biblical times, the greatest honor was to be covered in the dust of one's rabbi. The dust acquired in following along primitive roads and trails was a physical demonstration of what had been acquired through this unique rabbinic learning process. Children will always be covered with parents' dust. The question is, What kind of dust is it, dirt or gold dust?

The third and most important role that any father can fulfill in leadership in the home is that of leading the family in prayer and worship. This is perhaps the most neglected area of biblically Hebraic manhood. Most Christian men have abdicated from this leadership role and have surrendered, willingly or otherwise, their responsibility to the church and its professional clergy. In order to "bless and keep," men must maintain the most important part of human life in their own homes: relationship with the living God. Prayer and praise, study and devotion–all of these lead to the development and maintenance of a healthy, God-fearing home, with respectful, well-balanced, and maturing children.

Children learn faithfulness and integrity from the example of their parents, particularly their father. This begins in the honoring the sanctity of the marital relationship. What was a requirement for leaders in the earliest church must be the ideal to which every man aspires. In order to be a Christian spiritual leader, a man must be "the husband of one wife." The Greek text is literally translated, "a one-woman man."[45] This ideal of integrity is that each man be wholly devoted to one woman, his wife. The same can be said of wives who should be completely dedicated to their husbands; however, the lesson is focused on the man.

Jewish tradition suggests that women are inherently more spiritual than men; therefore, men need more discipline to live a godly life. If this is true, then the primary responsibility for maintaining the integrity of the marriage that is the foundation of the family is on the shoulders of the husband. There is no space in biblical faith for philandering or engaging in questionable dalliances with those who are not partners in the marriage. The ideal from the beginning was one man and one woman for life. Human failure has led to brokenness that fortunately is not irreparable. God is definitely the God of mercy who restores and even heals what has been shattered by sin. He also provides opportunity for a second chance. Heartbreaking situations can be avoided, however, if partners in marriage are careful to follow biblical guidelines for their conduct and not allow themselves to be swept up in the worldly promotion of vain "happiness" through emotional stimuli.

When men understand their God-given roles and learn the discipline of walking with God in fulfilling his instructions, they can live fulfilled, complete lives, lacking nothing. Maintaining the divine fatherhood principle of blessing and keeping and of teaching and leading is gratifying beyond any of the pleasures that hedonistic lifestyles can offer. The greatest legacy that a man can have is to have provided a godly home and to have reared God-fearing children. When his children rise up and honor him as a man of God, he has his ultimate reward and satisfaction.

BIBLICALLY HEBRAIC WOMANHOOD

Throughout profane history and in most of ecclesiastical history, womanhood has been defined in categories that have little resemblance to the biblically Hebraic model. Confucius expressed the Eastern perspective on women when he observed that because "men must have mothers . . . women are a necessary evil."[46] For the Buddhist woman there are eighteen special hells, but if she lives virtuously through 1,500 rebirths she may be born as a boy and at last reach *Nirvana* (nothingness).[47] Muslim women are trapped in an abusive system fraught with polygamy and serial divorce.

The ancient Greek philosophers, on whose thinking Western civilization is founded, considered women to be inherently evil. Aristotle, the high priest of Greek rationalism, considered woman to be little more than a deformed man, physically, mentally, and emotionally, going so far as to declare that "there is no virtue in women."[48] Plato believed that if a man were sufficiently evil during his lifetime he would be reincarnated as a woman.[49] Greek men were gynophobic and misogynistic. Many philosophers preferred pederastic relations to heterosexual relations because they worshipped the male body. In their thinking women served only the function of procreation, and contact with them should be limited.

At the time of its initial move toward Hellenization and Latinization, the Christian church abandoned biblical roles for women and adopted models from Hellenic, Latin, and pagan cultures, most of which have been demeaning at best and downright diabolical at worst. Because it adopted its view of womanhood from Greek categories, the Gentilized church has considered women as inherently less spiritual and more susceptible to sin than men. Entrenched male ecclesiastical bureaucracies have imprisoned Christian women behind demands for silence and submission through a church doctrine and polity grounded in the prejudice and/or ignorance of self-serving leaders and "substantiated" by misinterpreted and misapplied Holy Scripture.

During the twentieth century Western women began to find release from their bondage to male domination through various political movements; however, the pendulum swung from one extreme to the other forcing upon "liberated" women roles with which they have not been comfortable and removing from them roles and functions that they should have maintained. The result is confusion in womanhood and a significant lessening of feminine self-worth in many areas. When individuals take on roles for which they have not been designed or abandon roles for which they were designed, emotional chaos results.

Just as the church has presided over the emasculation of men, it has also been party to the disparaging and limitation of women. When early Greek and Latin church fathers sought to syncretize the philosophies of the Greeks with the Hebraic teaching of Jesus and the apostles, they succeeded in incorporating perverted Hellenic philosophical musings regarding women into the very doctrine and polity of the church. As a result, rather than being held in esteem as they were in ancient Hebraic culture, women have been viewed as second-class citizens of the kingdom of God. They have been characterized as being inferior to men in mental ability and spirituality. Their fecundity and materialism have been viewed as curses and traps to draw men of God away from a truly spiritual life. Demands for celibacy in the priesthood of the Western church were founded on these non-biblical ideas.

It is exceedingly shameful that the "liberation" of women has occurred through secular and political pressures rather than through the leading of the church. If the church had maintained its Hebraic foundations, Christian women would never have been subjected to such deplorable conditions and status. Because it abandoned its biblically Hebraic matrix, the church was able to read into Holy Scripture the perverse ideas of the pagan cultures to which they had been commissioned to carry the gospel. Though some more liberal, socially sensitive movements in Christianity have been supportive of efforts toward the liberation of women, much of conservative Christianity has plodded along, clinging tenaciously to age-old, non-biblical and even anti-biblical definitions of womanhood and feminine roles.

It is a wonder that the church has survived the pernicious ideas that have emasculated male believers and have imprisoned female believers in chains of bondage and submission. Needless to say, it is time for a revolution to occur in Christianity. The radical reformation of the sixteenth century needs to be taken to another level. Commitment to the Word of God rightly divided means commitment to exegeting Holy Scripture so that its intended meaning is understood, not a meaning that one wants to read into the text. It also means that Holy Scripture can only be understood when it is returned to the history and culture of the people who received it and to whom it first applied. When the biblically Hebraic mindset is brought to bear on the issue of feminine roles, some clear insights emerge.

In order to understand proper roles for women today, the most ancient texts describing womanhood must be revisited. It helps to begin at the beginning. Biblical woman was not a divine afterthought, nor was she formed from male spare parts. She was never intended to be a part of male chattel, a possession to be bought and sold. She was never designed to be a servant forced to function in silence and submission. She was never inferior either physically, intellectually, psychologically, or spiritually. And none of these traditional views of womanhood emerged as a result of the fall in the Garden of Eden.

Woman was designed by God to be a perfect counterpart for man. She was not a different creation. She was a power equal to him, lacking in nothing. She was to be a partner in a mutually supportive relationship that would provide balance and well-being for both man and woman. She was made from the same substance as man. The only difference between man and woman was one of function, of role. In Jewish understanding, while man provides physical strength and provision, the woman provides psychological strength and support.

Whereas man was to be provider through his work, woman was to be nurturer through her gift for relationship. Even a woman's anatomy clearly defines her role. She is equipped to nurture life in its most vulnerable stage. The womb around which God constructed woman is the safest place in the world for a human being for the first nine months of its existence. Subsequent to birth, the still helpless infant is nurtured at its mother's breasts, another clear difference between female and male physiologies.

Both of these anatomical features that are unique to womanhood have been elevated in Hebraic thinking to signify characteristics of God himself. In Hebrew, one of the words for divine mercy, רַחַם (*racham*),[50] is from the same root as the word for womb, רֶחֶם (*rechem*).[51] The extent of God's mercy is clearly manifest in the attention that a woman's body gives to a developing fetus. Likewise, women's breasts are paralleled in God's nature of providing sustenance to his helpless children. One of the significant names of God, *El Shaddai* (the Almighty), may be connected with the Hebrew word for breast שַׁד (*shad*).[52] The very idea, then, that women are somehow inherently evil either because of their physiological features or their psychological orientation is perverse and should be banished forever from the language and the thinking of the church. Indeed, Christians would do well to adopt the Jewish understanding that women are inherently more spiritual than men because they better reflect the qualities of the Divine through their manifestations of protective tender mercy and nurturing loving kindness.

Women's role in nurturing is augmented by the fact that

they are gifted in verbal expression, able to affirm and strengthen relationships. They are also far more in touch with their emotions than are their male counterparts.[53] Feminine hearts are more easily touched with human suffering, and they generally manifest greater altruism than do males. This quality has been honored in the Jewish community and in the Hebraic heritage on which Jewish understanding was based. The ancient Greeks, on the other hand, associated excessive emotion entirely with women and even coined the word *hysteria* from the Greek word for womb, *hystera*. This was but a further manifestation of the dim view of womanhood held in Greek male society that valued rationalism and general absence of emotions above all. Even today medical definitions of hysteria assert that this psychological condition is "a nervous affection, *occurring almost exclusively in women*, in which the emotional and reflex excitability is exaggerated" (emphasis added).[54]

Because the church incorporated Greek philosophical understandings of femininity into its doctrine and polity, it failed to realize the importance of feminine emotion to the health and well-being of marriage, home, and society. Because women were emotional, they were disqualified from important functions in church and society that demanded the "clear head" of male rationalism. As a result the emotional qualities of womanhood have not been encouraged and in some instances have been frowned upon and excoriated. The church has suffered a degree of impoverishment by not recognizing these qualities as a divine counterbalance to male perspectives both in the home, in the church, and in society.

A woman is designed by God to nurture, and not just to nurture children. She extends her nurturing nature to a protective stance toward her husband and her home. She was designed by God to be a qualified support to her husband in a sense parallel with that in which God is the helper of his people. She also possesses the divine gift for making a home, what has been called the nesting instinct. Woman seeks security in a protected environment for herself, for her husband, and for her children. More than mere instinct, this is a divine impartation of grace into the feminine spirit. The desire and ability to make a home are unique talents that God has given *sui generis* to womankind.

In the Talmud, Rabbi Yossi suggested that the words *wife* and *home* are synonymous.[55] A woman's role as a homemaker is more than just the fulfillment of a biological urge. It is a God-inspired endowment, for the blessings she imparts to the home are more than natural; they are spiritual as well. "A pious wife, living modestly within her domestic circle, is like the holy altar, an atoning power for the household," the sages of Israel declare.[56] Rabbi Samson Raphael Hirsch made this observation on the feminine talent for homebuilding: "A whole combination of knowledge, insight, abilities, and skills as well as moral virtue and spiritual excellence make up the art of the home builder."[57]

Militant feminism has decried the "homemaker" role and has so equated it with "slave" that the modern, liberated woman has generally disassociated herself from this title. Home economics, once a course for girls in high schools, is virtually nonexistent. Today's females want to be more than a homemaker. They've "come a long way, baby!" The truth is, however, that those women who neglect their God-given feminine gift for creating and maintaining the safe haven of the home will only suffer present disillusionment and regrets in later life.

A contemporary poster underscores the much-maligned homemaker's importance to the home, society, and the world. Titled "The Most Creative Job in the World," it says, "Taste, fashion, decorating, recreation, education, transportation, psychology, cuisine, designing, literature, medicine, handicraft, art, horticulture, economics, government, community relations, pediatrics, geriatrics, entertainment, maintenance, purchasing, direct mail, law, accounting, religion, energy, and management. Anyone who can handle all of those has to be somebody special. She is. She's a homemaker."[58]

While a woman's primary role of nurturer is manifest in the creation and maintenance of the home, roles for womanhood are in no way limited to the confines of the home. While the home should be a woman's priority, there are virtually no limits on the endeavors in which women can be engaged outside the home. Indeed, Jewish tradition suggests that a husband should encourage his wife to have interests outside the home. Husbands should invest their resources and personal energies in helping their wives find fulfillment both in the home and outside the home.

One need only look at the activities that brought honor to the woman of valour in Proverbs 31 to see the many endeavors which a woman may undertake. This priceless wife of virtue was skilled in creating objects from fibers and cloth. She was in the importing business, acquiring food from far-flung places. She was skilled with cuisine production and serving. She was a real estate developer and a vintner. She was a successful businesswoman. She was a philanthropist. She was a wise and faithful teacher. She had acquired wealth. In all, she was as successful outside the home as she was inside the family sanctuary. Whatever she did outside the home, however, was done in the interest of making her home more secure and happy.

To determine roles appropriate for women in today's world, one need only look at those that they fulfilled in biblical times with God's approval and blessing. Miriam was a divinely gifted teacher (the definition of the scriptural word *prophetess*).[59] Sarah is said by the Jewish people to have been a greater prophetess than Abraham was a prophet. Deborah was a judge in Israel, one of the highest leadership positions in the society of her time.[60] Esther was the queen of the world's most powerful dominion.[61]

This tradition that assigned women important roles in the community and in the exercise of religion in the Hebrew Scriptures was continued in the earliest Christian church.

This was in complete continuity with the Hebraic tradition and in contradistinction to the Hellenic tradition that later infected and infested the church with anti-biblical postures toward women. Philip's daughters were teachers (prophetesses).[62] Priscilla was the more prominent teacher in a wife-and-husband team, demonstrated by the fact that her name is mentioned before Aquila's.[63] Phebe was a minister (deaconess) of the Cenchrean church who was commissioned to transact church business in Rome.[64] Junia was an outstanding apostle.[65] Women were leaders of house churches in early Christianity.[66] What can women now do in society and church? Whatever they did in Bible times with God's approval. It's that simple![67]

It is a great shame on the church of history and today that severe limitations have been imposed upon women both in societal and ecclesiastical roles because of the infiltration of Hellenism into the church. Instead of maintaining the pure faith of Jesus and the apostles that was solidly grounded in the Hebraic heritage of their ancestors, the Gentile church has imported alien ideas into its doctrine and polity that have brought disillusionment to one half of its constituency and unrealistic responsibility to its other half. Now is the time to go back to the Book and restore biblically Hebraic womanhood.

Biblically Hebraic Children

The roles of children in society have changed rapidly and significantly in recent times, with various children's rights movements reacting to flagrant examples of child abuse with ever-increasing demands for children to be equal in rights and roles with adults. While child abuse is unthinkable in biblical categories, children are placed in a posture of protection and submission to their parents that does not confuse lines of authority and provides emotional and physical security that children need above all else.

In biblically Hebraic thinking, children are to be celebrated. "Children are a gift of the LORD. The fruit of the womb is a reward," the Scriptures declare.[68] When the very first human baby was born, his mother's reaction was, "I have acquired a man from the LORD."[69] The Bible even suggests that one who has many children is blessed.[70] Children are not a necessary evil or an unnecessary inconvenience. When conceived in the security of a believing family, they are considered to be holy unto God.[71] Parents should be diligent to surround their children with love similar to the way in which the divine Father envelops his children in his love.

Parents are responsible to provide love and security for their children, and, in turn, children are responsible for honoring their parents. This is the basis for the second of familial relationships that follows the first relationship, marriage itself. While children are not joined together with parents in the oneness that marriage inherently manifests, they still share a sacred relationship that is akin to no other interpersonal human interaction. They are genetically, emotionally, and spiritually a composite of what their parents are.

Parents are responsible for teaching their children. As a matter of fact, the Hebrew word for parent, *horeh*, is closely related to the word for teacher, *moreh*, and both come from the root word *yarah*, an archery term that means to hit the target. The word *Torah* also comes from this same root and means instruction (not "law" as it has been mistranslated in most English versions of the Scriptures). The Torah is God's instruction for his children, his set of guidelines for successful living.

One of the specific reasons that Abraham was chosen to be God's blessing channel to all the families of the earth was the fact that God knew Abraham would "command his children and his household after him to keep the way of the LORD by doing righteousness and justice."[72] Likewise, God's commandment to Israel was that parents should teach his instructions "diligently to your children," and the first place in which this exercise of parental teaching was to be established was "when you sit in your home."[73] The home, then, has primacy in education and is the locus for spiritual and emotional maturation.

Family teaching responsibilities begin with the mother, who, according to Hebraic understanding, instructed infants until they were weaned.[74] Then, the father was to the assume leadership in joining the mother to instruct the child until it reached puberty. Finally, the child was to be educated by the teachers and rabbis. Both the mother and the father's instructions to their children are important. "My son, heed the discipline of your father, and do not forsake [the law] of your mother . . . keep your father's commandment; do not forsake your mother's teaching."[75] A prime example of this home schooling is Timothy who was trained from infancy in the Scriptures by his mother Eunice and grandmother Lois.[76] Teaching, then, is a responsibility upon parents throughout their children's infancy, adolescence, and early adult life.

This instruction focuses both on the Word of God and on what has been termed "secular" education or learning to acquire job skills or a means of livelihood. This education may take place in formal schools; however, such institutions never relieve parental responsibility to be the primary educators of their children. Home schooling is not, therefore, a supplementary training mechanism in Jewish life, both for spiritual and secular understanding. The home is the primary venue and vehicle for all education, and all other teaching entities are supplementary to family tutelage.

Both of these areas of instruction are designed to fulfill the biblical imperative: "Train up a child in the way he should go."[77] The emphasis in this passage is upon the way the *child* should go, not the way in which the *parent* would have the child go. The Jewish understanding of this instruction is that it is incumbent upon parents to discern what gift, vision, and ambition a child has and then to work at providing instruction that will help the child to excel in fulfilling that goal. Children will not necessarily have the same preferences and skills as their parents. Each child is different, and each one's individuality must be respected and encouraged. If God wanted children to be perfect replicas of their parents, he would have instituted cloning rather than childbirth. Parents who are wise, therefore, will not demand that their children live out parental fantasies but rather will encourage and equip them to pursue their own aspirations.

Parents must provide for their children. They must maintain the essentials of life: food, clothing, and shelter. They are responsible for maintaining a secure environment in which children can feel safe and loved. Wise parents will sacrifice their own pleasures for the health and welfare of their children, and they will be abundantly rewarded for having done so both in this life and in the world to come.

Part of the security that children need is maintained by parental discipline. Parents must establish definite boundaries for their children's conduct, and they must reinforce those boundaries continually. Children without borders are insecure, and their insecurity will manifest itself in various unsavory ways, both in childhood and in later life. Many parents are afraid to enforce conformity to family boundaries and rules for fear of alienating their children. "They won't love me," parents moan, excusing the permissiveness that is rooted in their inability to discipline themselves so they can, in turn, discipline their children.

In order to be effective, discipline must be immediate, definitive, and final. It must have the impact of the applied rod of historical discipline. Vacillation will create insecurity and demands for further leniency and will lead to eventual disillusionment and rebellion. Corporeal punishment is an available option that may be a final resort. Some in modern societies discount the value of physical punishment and even seek to bring the weight of the law against parents who employ it. The Bible, however, makes the option available. Solomon observed that "the rod of correction imparts wisdom, but a child left to himself disgraces his mother,"[78] and the wise man noted that "he who spares the rod hates his son, but he who loves him is careful to discipline him."[79] The ideal, however, is the use of other means of discipline with the same finality as corporeal punishment.[80]

In exercising discipline, however, parents should always remember biblical injunctions against being overbearing or vicious. "Fathers, do not provoke your children to anger, but bring them up in the discipline and instruction of the Lord."[81] Jewish sages teach that it is forbidden to be too exacting with children regarding a parent's honor. Instead, parents should be forgiving, even minimizing or overlooking children's mistakes whenever possible.[82] Christian parents should be careful to exercise the tender mercies and loving kindness that the heavenly Father has demonstrated to them in passing over their sins and welcoming them into his parental embrace.

Children are required to honor their parents. One tenth of the Decalogue is devoted to this precept.[83] Honor for parents is just as important to societal well-being as prohibitions against murder and theft. Philo of Alexandria observed, "Who could be more truly called benefactors than parents in relation to their children? First, they have brought them out of non-existence . . . to nurture and later to educate, body and soul, so that they may have not only life, but a good life."[84] Honor is a lifelong filial responsibility toward parents.

Children may not always agree with their parents, nor are they required to do so. They are, however, required to *honor* their parents. This honor means obedience in childhood, and it means respect and care when they are adults and their parents are advanced in age. No one is permitted to circumvent his responsibility to honor his parents. Jesus himself excoriated those who sought to hide behind the temple as a means of avoiding their duty to respect and care for their aged parents.[85] Solomon declared that any man who "curses his father or mother, his lamp will be snuffed out in pitch darkness."[86] On the other hand, one who honors his parents is assured long life in the first commandment with promise.[87] Paul summed up children's responsibility very succinctly: "Children, obey your parents in the Lord, for this is right."[88]

Children should be taught from a tender age the responsibility that they have to the family, to the community, and to the world at large. Innate selfishness must be addressed and removed from the child's psyche. One good way to accomplish this is to provide opportunities for children to give to others some of what is given to them. In Jewish homes, a *tzedekah* box is prominently displayed, and children are encouraged to place coins in the box to be given to those in society who are less fortunate. The box is termed *tzedekah* (righteousness, i.e. charity) because giving to the poor is an act of righteousness in obedience to God's commanded that one love his neighbor as himself[89] and give to the poor.[90] When a child comes to understand that he is not the center of the universe, that other family members have needs, and that one is responsible even to help those beyond the family circle, he is set on the path of *tikkun olam* (restoring the world).

Children also should be blessed on a regular basis in the security of the family sanctuary. A host of biblical blessings is available to discriminating parents who understand the power of the Word of God and want to take on themselves the role of family priesthood that speaks God's benedictions into the lives of their children.

Children who are reared in the biblically Hebraic model for childhood will be set on a path toward relationship with God and will adopt strong family values that then will be passed on to the next generation. Biblically Hebraic childhood is a blessed state and an important part of the family sanctuary.

ESTABLISHING SECURE BOUNDARIES

Boundary definition is an essential part of family *halachah*. Beyond outlining proper roles for family members, secure boundaries must be established for every home. The individual family has considerable help in this matter, for the Holy Scriptures have circumscribed human existence with many very clear borders. One need only look in the Bible to find the Creator's design and maintenance specifications. Each family should be unreservedly committed to the divine inspiration, absolute authority, and clear reliability of the Bible as the guidebook for human existence. When there is one recognized source for absolutes, establishing boundaries is greatly facilitated.

Secondary assistance in family *halachah* is found in worshipping communities. There is wisdom in Solomon's observation that "where no wise direction is, people fall; but in the multitude of counsellors there is safety."[91] The wise king also noted that "plans fail for lack of counsel, but with many advisers they succeed."[92] It is simply wise for families to seek the input of a trusted community of believers into their personal and familial lives. Corporate leaders in the body of Christ are commissioned with the responsibility of establishing *halachah* for those in their charge.[93] Jesus required the people to observe the instructions of those who sat "in Moses' seat," the spiritual leaders of the Jewish community.[94] Believers will remember and even obey leaders who have spoken God's Word to them and have demonstrated righteousness through their godly lifestyles.[95]

Guidelines may vary from community to community and from ethnicity to ethnicity, for the divine principles of Scripture must be contextualized into every corporate situation. This is the reason that God has given latitude for expression and fulfillment of his purposes. Paul most eloquently described this divine pluriformity by noting that various members of the Christian fellowship were at liberty to function in different ways, but no one was to judge another.[96] As Paul observed, each family and individual must be "fully persuaded in his own mind." What may be considered acceptable etiquette in one place may be entirely unacceptable elsewhere. It is important, therefore, that families conform as much as possible to the lifestyles of their communities as long as those lifestyles do not violate the clear instructions of Holy Scripture.[97]

Beyond those things in family life that are specifically addressed by the Word of God and in addition to suggestions for proper behavior in a specific community, there are other aspects of family life that must be judged, set forth, and maintained within the confines of the family. Parents together must determine what is acceptable deportment within their own family. They must live by their own rules first. Then they must teach their children conformity to these guidelines, enforcing the family decorum. Again, these familial preferences can be wide and varied, as long as they do not violate biblical precepts. What one family may be convicted to do may not be the same as what another family may consider essential. As with tolerance for congregational differences on protocols, diversities of emphases in various families must be respected and honored. True unity in the community of faith is that which maintains cohesion while encouraging diversity. Individual families should, however, remember Hillel's advice: "Do not separate yourself from the community."[98] Isolation from the community of believers is an invitation to deception and disaster.

Just as Israel's deliverance was effected one family at a time with a lamb for each household,[99] so each family must take responsibility for its own spiritual condition and its fulfillment of the things of God. Like Judah in Nehemiah's time, each family must build the part of the corporate wall of protection that is in front of its own house.[100] Security in the family sanctuary results from having constructed solid fortifications, establishing parameters and perimeters for right conduct within the home that shut out incursions of foreign and injurious elements from without. Boundaries of family *halachah* help make the home sanctuary a true retreat to safety and sanctity.

Commitment to God's Word with family *halachah* builds a hedge of defense around the home. The living Word becomes a sentinel at the gate of the family sanctuary, much like the *mezuzah* that stands guard duty at the doors of Jewish homes because they have literally fulfilled God's command and have written his instructions on the doorposts of their homes. Family *halachah* guards the gates, providing security for the family within and protection from the enemy without.

ESTABLISHING HALACHAH

Family *halachah* is vital to the family sanctuary. The right and responsibility of each family to establish its own *halachah* must be both respected and encouraged. First, it allows the home to be the locus for spiritual development as it was designed to be. Second, it keeps family members from abdicating their own responsibilities in favor of community leaders. Third, it promotes commitment to the individual family from all its members, both parents and children. Fourth, it encourages maturity in that it requires individual responsibility and accountability. Fifth, it positions each family for its own face-to-face encounter with God, a return to the Edenic sanctuary.

Joshua summed up the beauty and strength of proper attendance to family *halachah* this way: "As for me and my house, we will serve the LORD."[101] In the final analysis, it is a family-by-family decision. The way in which one should walk is established in the lifestyle that is lived in the family sanctuary, family *halachah*.

[1] Steven G. Post, "Splendor of Love," in *Nature, Man, and God* (Dallas: Southern Methodist University Press, 1994), p. 17.

[2] Genesis 2:24.

[3] Genesis 1:28.

[4] Erasmus, "In Praise of Marriage" in *Erasmus on Women*, ed. Erick Rumnell (Toronto: University of Toronto Press, 1996), p. 59.

[5] Galatians 5:19; Exodus 20:14. Adultery includes any extramarital act of sexual intercourse, whether heterosexual, homosexual, or zoophilic. Fornication involves any premarital act of sexual intercourse.

[6] Malachi 2:14-15.

[7] Ephesians 6:4.

[8] Ignaz Maybaum, "Tradition that Is Living" in *Marriage and the Jewish Tradition*, Stanley R. Brav, ed. (New York: Philosophical Library, 1951), p.54-55.

[9] In male-dominated societies, polygamy is almost universally manifest as polygyny, not polyandry. It seems that it is acceptable for men to have

multiple wives but unacceptable for women to have multiple husbands! Islam's teaching and that of various indigenous societies is clearly in violation of God's original intent for marriage. Even the examples of polygyny in Hebrew history were not ordered by God, even though they may have been tolerated as a result of societal norms.

[10] Matthew 19:8.

[11] Matthew 19:6.

[12] Jesus decried the liberal view that permitted divorce for any reason; however, he said that divorce and remarriage are permitted in cases of marital infidelity (Matthew 19:9). Paul agreed that marital partners were free to divorce and remarry in cases of abandonment (1 Corinthians 7:15) and suggested that individuals should remain in the matrimonial state in which they came to faith in Jesus (1 Corinthians 7:27-31).

[13] Malachi 2:16.

[14] Demosthenes, *Against Neaera 122*.

[15] Jacob Weinstein, "Better Than Romantic Love" in *Marriage and the Jewish Tradition*, Stanley R. Brav, ed. (New York: Philosophical Library, 1951), p. 205.

[16] Genesis 24:67.

[17] Ephesians 5:25.

[18] Albert Henry Newman, *Manual of Church History*, Vol 1 (1986), p. 366.

[19] Tertullian. *De exhortatione Castitatis*, ix.

[20] 1 Corinthians 7:2-5, New International Version.

[21] Michael Kaufman, *Love, Marriage, and Family in Jewish Law and Tradition* (Northvale, N.J.: Jason Aronson, 1992), p. 119.

[22] Proverbs 5:18-19.

[23] Genesis 2:24.

[24] David M. Feldman, *Health and Medicine in the Jewish Tradition* (New York: Crossroads, 1987), p. 63.

[25] *Eruvin* 100b.

[26] Deuteronomy 24:5, New International Version.

[27] Michael Kaufman, p. 227.

[28] Babylonian Talmud, *Yevamot* 62a.

[29] Ibid., *Temurah* 17a; *Bava Batra* 10b; *Berachot* 60a.

[30] Maimonides, *Book of Holiness*, section 9.

[31] Michael Kaufman, p. 214.

[32] Ephesians 5:21.

[33] Charles Bryant-Abraham, "On the Restoration of Biblical Womanhood to the Christian Believer," unpublished paper, p. 3.

[34] Genesis 21:12.

[35] Genesis 3:19.

[36] Genesis 2:15.

[37] Numbers 6:24.

[38] Genesis 3:19.

[39] Genesis 3:19.

[40] Exodus 20:9.

[41] Ephesians 5:25.

[42] John 3:16.

[43] Matthew 4:19; 9:9; 19:21.

[44] 1 Corinthians 11:1; 2 Thessalonians 3:7-9.

[45] 1 Timothy 3:2.

[46] W. Dallmann, *The Battle of the Bible with the "Bibles"* (St. Louis: Concordia, 1926), p. 36.

[47] Russell P. Prohl, *Woman in the Church* (Grand Rapids: Wm. B. Eerdmans Publishing Company, 1957), p. 50.

[48] Aristotle, *Generation of Animals*, 2.737a:27.

[49] Plato, *Timaeus*, 91a.

[50] cf. Genesis 43:14.

[51] cf. Genesis 29:31.

[52] The majority of scholarship agrees that the word *Shaddai* comes from the Akkadian word for mountain, indicating God's sufficiency and strength (cf. David's statement in Psalm 121:1, "I will lift up mine eyes unto the hills, from whence cometh my help"). Some, however, have suggested that *Shaddai* is associated with the Hebrew word for breast, indicating God's complete sufficiency to nurture his children.

[53] Though from a Hebraic perspective men are free to express emotion, women are more in touch with and more expressive of their emotions. Though the quintessential Jewish men, King David and Jesus, both wept (1 Samuel 30:4; Psalm 6:6; John 11:35; Luke 19:41), it is a fact that women shed tears more easily than men.

[54] cf. *Mirriam Webster's Medical Dictionary*, quoted on the web page: http://dictionary.reference.com/search?q=hysteria.

[55] Babylonian Talmud, *Yoma* 2a.

[56] *Midrash Tanhuma, Yayishlah*, 6.

[57] Samson Hirsch, *The Wisdom of Mishle* (Jerusalem, Feldheim Press, 1966), p. 246.

[58] Quoted in Michael Kaufman, p. 250.

[59] Exodus 15:20.

[60] Judges 4:4.

[61] Esther 2:17.

[62] Acts 21:8-9.

[63] Acts 18:26.

[64] Romans 16:1.

[65] Romans 16:7.

[66] There were congregations in the house of Chloe (1 Corinthians 1:11), Lydia (Acts 16:40), Mark's mother (Acts 12:12), Nympha (Colossians 4:15), and Priscilla (1 Corinthians 16:19). John also wrote his second epistle to the "elect lady" (2 John 1:1). The term *elect lady* in Greek was *eklekta*, which likely indicated that this woman was an ordained (elected or appointed) minister.

[67] This is consistent with God's immutability. "I am the LORD, I change not," he declared in Malachi 3:6. "Jesus Christ the same, yesterday, and today, and forever" is a cardinal principle of divine immutability established in Hebrews 13:8. Anything that God has ever approved must in some form still be acceptable to him, including guidelines for human roles and behavior.

[68] Psalm 127:3, New American Standard Version.

[69] Genesis 4:1.

[70] Psalm 127:4-5.

[71] 1 Corinthians 7:14.

[72] Genesis 18:19, New American Standard Version.

[73] Deuteronomy 6:7.

[74] It should be noted that in ancient times infants were weaned at a much

later age than in the modern Western world. In current Chassidic Jewish tradition, a boy's hair is cut, and he is taken by his father to his first day at school on his third birthday, signifying the transition from babyhood into childhood.

[75] Proverbs 1:18; 6:20, *Tanakh* (Jewish Publication Society). The word *law* in brackets is a literal translation of the Hebrew *torah.*

[76] 2 Timothy 1:5; 3:15.

[77] Proverbs 13:24.

[78] Proverbs 22:6.

[79] Proverbs 29:15.

[80] Biblical instructions about corporeal punishment should be viewed in the light of the scriptural injunction that required "an eye for an eye and a tooth for a tooth." This *lex talionis* was to be interpreted and applied as a means of imposing fair monetary penalties for intentional or accidental injury, not a literal exacting of the commandment. Likewise, corporeal punishment should speak of the swiftness and finality of punishment and never be manifest as any form of child abuse.

[81] Ephesians 6:4, New American Standard Version.

[82] *Shulhan Aruch, Yoreh D'ah* 240:19.

[83] Exodus 20:12.

[84] Quoted in Michael Kaufman, p. 288.

[85] Mark 7:10-11.

[86] Proverbs 20:20, New International Version.

[87] Exodus 20:12; Ephesians 6:2. Longevity is not guaranteed in response to honoring one's parents; however, it is a divine promise.

[88] Ephesians 6:1.

[89] Leviticus 19:18.

[90] Proverbs 19:1, 7. For the Jewish people, giving to the less fortunate of society is done because of God's instructions, not because of pity or emotion. It is a part of the righteousness that is manifest in fulfilling the commandments, hence the term *tzedekah* for "charity."

[91] Proverbs 11:14, Jewish Publication Society Old Testament.

[92] Proverbs 15:22, New International Version.

[93] When Jesus said in Matthew 16:19 that whatever his disciples bound or loosed on earth would be bound or loosed in heaven, he was affirming their authority to bind upon or loose from believers those requirements that would benefit their spiritual lives. This was the same authority that Jesus recognized in the scribes and Pharisees who established Jewish *halachah.*

[94] Matthew 23:2-3.

[95] Hebrews 13:7,17.

[96] Romans 14:4-14.

[97] Families should avoid assembling in corporate fellowships where clear biblical teachings are being violated. Not insisting on family *halachah* in these situations is to invite being drawn into a cult and opening the family boundaries to all sorts of deception.

[98] Steven Carr Reuben, *Raising Jewish Children in a Contemporary World* (Rocklin, Calif.: Prima Publishing, 1992), p. 145.

[99] Exodus 12:3.

[100] Nehemiah 3:1-32.

[101] Joshua 24:15.

Chapter 8

Restoring the Family Sanctuary

The Church Is Going Home

For centuries, the Christian home has been dysfunctional in many ways because its original Hebraic foundations have been eroded by influences from Gentile philosophies and religious systems. In recent decades, it has suffered violent attack from secularists bent on redefining the family to accommodate politically correct tolerance for aberrations and perversions. Biblical family roles have been replaced in the public square through insidious, vicious attacks camouflaged as "values-clarification." The all-wise state knows what is best for society, and it inculcates and enforces the official, state-sponsored religion of secular humanism through its school systems, attacking and brainwashing the most vulnerable members of society, the children.

Millions of Christians are now seeking remedy for this malady. In large part, the church has been unable and perhaps unwilling to lead believers in finding the answer. For some eighteen centuries it has actually contributed to the problem by removing from the home its biblically Hebraic heritage, turning the focus from family to the institutional church. Instead of encouraging lay participation in extra-ecclesial study and worship in the context of the family, the official church produced a clergy-laity gap that eventually divided the church into two churches, the *ecclesia clerens* (the teaching church) and the *ecclesia audiens* (the listening church). With this innovation, performance-based Christianity became the official norm. Like their contemporaries who gathered in imposing, grandiose temples to witness the theatre of pagan rites, the laity of the church assembled in ever more magnificent cathedrals to view the spectacle of priestly performance that was increasingly veiled in mystery.

The result of this gradual shift of emphasis from the home to the church was and remains to this day a debilitation of the church body politic. One of the immediate results was the decline of learning in the areas where the church dominated. Learning became almost exclusively the province of the church and its professional clergy. Eventually, the masses became totally illiterate. With the church also assuming exclusive rights to worship experiences, the masses no longer worshipped in their homes. The result was an increase in superstition and dependence upon occasional "church" experiences for any sense of spirituality.

When renewal movements finally emerged both within and outside the official church, they did not address the problem that was debilitating the church: the virtual destruction of the family sanctuary. The clergy-laity gap remained intact with only minor adjustments. Church institutions and the clergy continued to be the focus of Christian activity. Spectator Christianity was maintained in one form or another and still remains the dominant form of religious expression in today's church.

GOING BACK IN ORDER TO GO FORWARD

Individuals who have a passion for more than a nominal Christian experience have grown restless in the face of ecclesiastical unresponsiveness to their need for intimacy with God.

Increasingly, they are turning to small groups and are meeting in homes for fellowship, study, and worship. Most of these represent the church's very best talent, its most dedicated members. They are searching for a spiritual reality that will build faith in their hearts and in their homes. Because they have not found answers in traditional institutional structures, believers have begun to assume responsibility for their own spiritual condition. The result has been the emergence of an indigenous home-church movement.

Returning the focus of Christian experience to the home has created a need for community fellowship and corporate worship experiences of like-minded people. The movement back to the family is crying out for leadership that encourages family worship and study while providing biblicallymandated opportunities for fellowship, study, and worship in the context of community. In reality, the church should be facilitating this refocus on the home and the family, restoring both to biblical perspectives. Church leaders should come to understand themselves as facilitators for individuals and families, equipping saints for works of ministry in every arena of life.[1]

A rethinking of both the church and the family must be undertaken if both are to survive the onslaught of secularist attack. It is time for in-depth analysis of theology's most neglected area of investigation: ecclesiology (the study of the church). What constitutes the church? How does it function? What is its purpose? These are issues that theologians and church leaders must face head on. Questions of what constitutes worship, fellowship, and service must also be answered. In short, Christianity must reexamine itself from within before it crumbles from within.

A return to the biblical models in which Jesus and the apostles lived their lives and expressed their devotion to the heavenly Father will empower the church to experience the profound growth that it enjoyed in its earliest formative days.

The Lord will add to the church daily in ever increasing numbers when it continues daily in fellowship, teaching, and prayers, breaking bread from house to house. The family sanctuary will never replace the corporate worshipping community. If encouraged to function in biblically Hebraic order, the home church will cause the corporate community of believers to experience explosive growth. Traditional high levels of recidivism among new converts to Christianity will be negated by returning the focus for discipleship and maturity to the family sanctuary. When the home is the locus for spiritual growth, everyone has a sphere of accountability, and the corporate community grows both qualitatively and quantitatively.

THE HOLISTIC HOME

For far too long, the lives of Christians, both as individuals and families, have been separated, bifurcated into two hemispheres, the spiritual and the secular. Influenced by neo-Platonism and residues of Gnosticism,[2] the church has reinforced this perspective by removing spiritual leadership from the home and assigning it almost exclusively to the church. This dualism has encouraged individuals and families to live in two realms, one spiritual, the other secular. More often than not, the spiritual sphere for them has been the church and the experiences they share periodically in church worship centers. The home, consequently, has generally been left by default in the secular domain. This perspective has made the home easy prey for the entertainment industry, and has allowed secularism to diminish and eliminate spiritual exercises.

When one bypasses the Americanization, Europeanization, Latinization, and Hellenization of Christianity and returns to the church's Hebraic foundations, dualism is no longer an option. Life cannot be dichotomized to allow different lifestyles and ethics in spiritual and secular realms. For the Hebrews, everything was spiritual, everything theological. From the mundane to the sublime, all aspects of life were to be lived under the purview of God's instructions. Everything was to be done to the glory of God.[3]

Family sanctuary is a sure cure for domestic violence, for how can one dare to manifest destructive behavior if the home is also recognized as a house of God? Hebraic holism does not permit areas of life to be off limits for God's instructions and proper, ethical conduct. The commandments of God apply in the home just as they apply in the church. They are just as viable in the public square and in the world of commerce as they are in the church.

When all of life is lived for God, the spiritual begins in the individual heart, then extends to the family, and finally reaches fullest flower in community. What is biblically mandated to be done in the corporate community of believers must first be done in individual hearts and then in individual families. Instead of a divisive dualism, believers experience a healthy holism. They are working in partnership with God in the Hebraic process of *tikkun olam* (restoration of the world), beginning with themselves, then with their families, and finally with their communities and the world. They are like Adam "keepers of the garden," the sanctuary of their own home.[4]

Impacting community and the world begins at home when the family sanctuary opens its sacred assembly to friends and extended family and even to strangers. Like Sarah's tent, the family sanctuary is a place for Hebraic hospitality. Bringing others into the sanctuary keeps it from becoming exclusive and elitist, from being introverted, turned in on itself. It adds strength from the blessing that others have to impart into the family and from the blessing that the family bestows upon others.

This is not merely an idyllic, utopian view of family. It is an opportunity to believe the ideal while experiencing the real. It is retreating into the sanctuary of God's instructions while facing the difficulties in life that result from fallen humanity. It is assuming responsibility for personal growth while maintaining the input of community and divinely appointed spiritual leaders. It is an effort to bring heaven to earth by involving God in every aspect of human existence.

CALLING TIME OUT

Wise Christians are learning to call time out. Enough is enough! It is time to retreat into the sanctuary of loving, affirming relationships. Once the family sanctuary is built and fortified as a place of refuge and strength, it is accessible to every member of the family. All one needs to do is to call time. When set times for family interaction have been established, quality time that has seemed so fleeting and unachievable becomes available and sufficient. If pressures mount or situations arise that do not conform to the family appointment calendar, one can call time out and retreat into the sanctuary for communion with God and family that brings renewal and fresh resolve to face life's challenges.

Wise Christian leaders are even calling time out from the excessive programs that have been devised to keep individuals and families involved in the church. They are learning to multiply their effective ministry by training and equipping heads of households who can, in turn, replicate the teaching and worship in their own homes, thereby strengthening the church exponentially. Rather than making involvement in church programs almost a requisite of salvation, they are insisting that families create time sanctuaries for their families and fully realize the blessings of God upon their homes.

Translocal leaders of the Christian community are also calling time out to rethink traditional Christianity and to stop the rat race of doing the same things over and over again. Insanity has been defined as continuing to do the same things that one has been doing all the while expecting a different outcome. If the results that the church is achieving are not acceptable–and they are not–it is time for spiritual leaders to yell, "Time out!" Leaders need to take a sabbatical for reflection and renewal on the task of restoring and strengthening the church's fundamental and founding unit, the family sanctuary.

It is also time for leaders to make appointments to consider how the old paths wherein is the good way can be restored.[5] It is time for church leaders to give careful consideration to rebuilding the holy city's walls, to closing up the breaches made by unrelenting attacks from the enemy.[6] It is time to restore the tent of David that has fallen into such disarray.[7] It is time to renew the faith once delivered to the saints.[8]

GOING HOME

The growing need for sanctuary in a world gone mad is driving more and more people into the one environment that they have the potential to control, their own homes. As societal insanity, fueled by moral failure, increasingly breeds sociopaths and psychopaths bent upon indiscriminate violence and seeks to suppress individual freedoms for religious expression, parents feel the need to cordon off space and erect barricades against perversion and emotional and physical threats. They are retreating with their children to the enduring sanctuary of the family.

There is rarely a more gratifying moment than being able to go back home after a long excursion to a distant place. Likewise, it is satisfying and spiritually rewarding to go back to the place where the church and the synagogue began, the family sanctuary. What began in a garden home and was more fully manifest in the tent of a family of faith reached full manifestation in the congregation of Israel. What was initiated in Jewish homes in Babylon was fully realized in the diverse and rich synagogues of both Judaea and the diaspora. What started in Jewish Christian homes during the Roman occupation came to full flower in the congregations of Christ throughout the world. Everything started with the family sanctuary.

Restoring biblically Hebraic concepts for family and home will bring renewal and health to modern manifestations of the family, the synagogue, and the church. Understanding that the home is a *mikdash me'at* (a temple in miniature) complete with a family altar and a functioning priesthood will revolutionize the life and ministry of the church, bringing a renewed and enduring vitality that will not be eroded by the short attention spans of the modern mind. Christians are coming to understand what is truly important in life: God and family. Increasing numbers are embracing the roots of Christian faith that are anchored deep in the soil of biblical Judaism.

The institution of the church is also headed home. In a quest for orthodoxy, some are stopping at Canterbury, Geneva, Wittenburg, Rome, or Constantinople. Many, however, are determined to go all the way back home–to Jerusalem and the Hebraic roots of their faith. When they reach the heights of that city of gold, they experience that swell of emotion that says, "I'm home!" And so they are–home where the Christian church had its beginnings, home where the faith destined for all nations began its trek around the world.

Now is the time for believers everywhere to follow the leading of the Holy Spirit to go back home. It is time to restore the one faith for all peoples, the Hebraic heritage of the prophets and sages and of Jesus and the apostles. Nowhere is this restoration more important than in the Christian home and family. It is time to stop bemoaning the onslaught of human and demonic forces against the Christian faith and start restoring health and vitality to the faith's most fundamental unit, the family. It is time to restore the family sanctuary. Men and women of vision are now declaring without reservation, "As for me and my house, we will serve the Lord." The church is going home, to the family sanctuary

[1] Ephesians 4:11-12.
[2] Platonic and Gnostic dualism teaches that the material is evil. The Bible teaches that everything is inherently good but can be used for evil.
[3] 1 Corinthians 10:31.
[4] Genesis 2:15.
[5] Jeremiah 6:15.
[6] Amos 9:11.
[7] Acts 15:15-16.
[8] Jude 1:3.

Index

S

T

U

V

W

Y